Victory
at
Video Poker

*and other video
games including
Video Blackjack,
Video Craps and
Video Keno*

Frank Scoblete

Bonus Books, Inc., Chicago

99   98   97   5   4   3   2

Library of Congress Catalog Card Number: 95-80263

International Standard Book Number: 1-56625-043-9

Bonus Books, Inc.
160 East Illinois Street
Chicago, Illinois 60611

Composition by Point West Inc., Carol Stream, IL

Printed in the United States of America

*This book is dedicated to
Susan, Tony, Melanie and Jason—
may you have victory in life!*

*And to the memory of
Phil Quattrocchi
and
Paul Cavalluzzi—
God is calling his own.*

Contents

"It was without a compeer among swindles.
It was perfect, it was rounded, symmetrical,
complete, colossal."
                                        —*Mark Twain*

Acknowledgements

This was a most difficult book to write because some of the greatest effort is not all that noticeable. It is contained in page after page of strategy decisions for the various video-poker machines that I describe. As such it was a painstaking, exhaustive effort that did not end in delightful prose but rather in prosaic, albeit important, lists. Still, I think this is the most complete and accurate book on all the video games currently being offered in today's casinos and as such I'm proud to have written it. Tired but proud.

For the video-poker sections I would especially like to thank Dr. James Schneider who did the computer studies for me. What we discovered was not news for us. There are certain video-poker strategies that work and certain video-poker machines that can be beaten. It was a reaffirmation of what other video-poker authors and computer scientists had already discovered. Still, it's nice to know that what others have said is indeed true and verifiable—*video poker can be beaten!*

The chapters on video craps and video blackjack owe much to my own book *Guerrilla Gambling: How to Beat the Casinos at Their Own Games!* Since the essential thrust of both these video games is the same as their table-game cousins, I have adapted and updated what I have written previously on these subjects. However, both games have video-variants not found in their table kin and these I have delineated and explained fully. I'd like to thank Howard T. Mann for helping me out with the video-keno chapter of the book.

And a special thanks to the following for helping me with this project: to the Captain and the beautiful A.P for their inspiration and insights; to Phil and Angela, the Bulletman and Bride of Bulletman, who allowed me to put some meat on the bare bones of video-poker strategy; to *Blackjack Forum's* great team of writers, including Dan Paymar, Allan Pell and Joel H. Friedman, whose insightful and well-written articles alerted me to the possibility of "rigged" machines. To Alan Tinker, who was the first person to tell me that video poker was worth looking into at a time in my gaming career when I was disdainful of anyone who went near a machine. Thanks, Alan. A whole book can trace its germination to a single moment: you joyously sitting at a video-poker machine at Binions Horseshoe and telling me that this was "one great game!"

1

Fate, Free Will, and a Flip of the Cards

From the moment our forebears postulated that there were forces in the universe greater than they, we as a species have been obsessed with our collective and individual fates. What does the future hold? Has it already been decided by a Divine Being or are we free to choose the various roads we will travel in this mortal realm? If there is a single God as most Western religions teach, and if this God is omnipotent, omnipresent, and omniscient, does the fact that *He* knows the future mean that we lowly humans have no choice in its formation and structure? When the Divine Dealer gives us life's cards, do we get to freely play the hand we are dealt—discarding some cards, requesting some others? Or must we stay with a pat hand—even if it's a loser? Are we free to make choices such a Divine Entity has *not* foreseen? Or are we doomed the way a tragic character in a Greek play is doomed from the very opening of the very first scene? Are we deluded by our own hope—we think we are making choices but in reality these choices are but illusions?

Nor has our greater scientific enlightenment given us any greater insight into the matter of fate vs. free will. The same questions have only been restructured with a new, more scientific vocabulary. Are we creatures whose every thought, word, and deed is determined by a synergistic combination of our genetic natures and our environmental nurturing? In computerese: are our futures utterly and universally formatted by our genetic and environmental pasts? Or are we creatures for whom *will* is the determining factor in our fate? Can what we *will* to be actually become what will be?

If this latter assumption, nay hope, is correct, then we humans have some say in how we play the hand that is dealt us in this life. We have some freedom. Yes, it is limited. Even the greatest exponents of the free will of man recognize that some things are beyond our capacity for choice. Yet what was beyond the choice of a man 200 years ago—such as flying in the air faster and higher than any bird that has ever been—is not beyond our scope today. We may not have been dealt wings but we have *willed* them!

And that's the fundamental difference between slot machines and video-poker machines.

The slot machine is a fate-oriented device. You put your money in and the god-in-the-machine—that is, the random-number generator—selects what symbols will appear and you are then informed of your fate. The only choices a slot player makes are tangential to but not inherent in the machine: how much will I play, how long will I play and, most important of all, what machine will I play. It is tantamount to deciding which of the many skyscrapers in New York you'll jump off. Once you've decided, the only thing left is an uninterrupted plunge to the ground.

Not so with the video-poker and video-blackjack player. Both games are rife with choices. You can't choose what hand you'll be dealt initially but you sure as heaven can decide how to play it.

I believe it is this "free-will" factor that has caused the phenomenal growth of video-poker machines in American casinos since they were first introduced in the 1970's. Unlike the deterministic slots, the video-poker machines offer the hope of a better tomorrow. With slots, the machine gives you the decision and you have to live with it. But in video poker it is different. Got a zilch hand? Discard it and draw another. The video-poker machine stimulates our basic human emotions of hope, anticipation, joy, and disappointment. In addition, the video-poker machine gives us some responsibility for the results of our choices. On the slots you are not responsible for what eventuates because the god-in-the-machine determines everything and merely informs you of its *a priori* decision. But in video poker, you are partially responsible because *your* decisions help to determine your future—especially your long-term future.Thus, the character of your play will determine your ultimate economic fate. Character is fate, as some Greek philosophers contended.

When you know that you have some responsibility for the decision about to be rendered, you are engaged on many levels. Why? Because *you* are on the line. Intellectually you know that you must make a choice and that choices have consequences. Emotionally you know the joy or sorrow that success or failure will bring. Nothing can quite compete with that delicious sensation of receiving four cards to a royal flush on the initial hand. As you discard the junk card and press the draw button, your heart pounds with anticipation and, yes, dread. In the back of your mind, in some adrenaline-soaked reverie that skirts the surface of your waking consciousness, you picture yourself as attendants come over to pay you your huge win. In a stop-action, mental motion picture, you watch and experience the crowd of people who will come over to slap your back and congratulate you on your good fortune—a fortune that you know you deserve because you made the right choice.

Of course, it almost always ends in disappointment—as do so many things in real and reel life. And this you know, too, that more than likely you will be disappointed. You won't get the royal flush. And you know that usually you don't get anything for your efforts but the lingering aftereffects of that momentary adrenaline rush when all things were in the malleable future instead of in the concrete past. Sometimes fate will throw you a bone and you'll double up one of your high cards to break even and live to play another day—in some cases that is. But you were involved; you were engaged, and you got to make some choices. All this passes in lightning-time through your nerve fibers as you press the DEAL-DRAW button to create the fate that your choices will help to seal.

The Game of Choice

Video poker is not just a game of choices but *the* game of choice for most new casino players. Although no scientific survey has been done to confirm my assertion, the number of video-poker machines being manufactured and distributed to various casinos around the country (and the world) indicates that it is the game of choice for a substantial minority of all casino players and a growing majority of machine players. More than 50 percent of the floor space reserved for machines in most casinos is taken up by video-poker machines. While most casinos do not distinguish between video poker (or other video games) and slots in their published win and hold figures (all of them falling under the generic "slot" label), most of the casino executives I spoke to agreed that video-poker players are the fastest-growing segment of the playing public.

One Las Vegas slot manager had this to say: "Video poker of all varieties is the most popular form of machine play. As we draw up our plans for future placement of new machines in our expanded floor space, we are running 70/30 video poker to traditional slots. The traditional slots have a huge following but the video-poker generation is coming of age. Right now it's close but in the next 20 years I expect that video poker will outperform the traditional slots and dominate the casino landscape."

Some casino personnel made a point of alerting me to consider who plays what kind of machine as one explanation for the growing popularity of video poker. Stated one casino executive in Atlantic City: "Look at who plays video poker and who plays slots and you'll see that the majority of your slot players are older. These are people who have been coming to casinos for years and are in the habit of slot playing. These same people, the majority of whom are women, rejected playing table games in the past, for whatever reason. The video-poker players on average are younger. Many of the older video-poker players are former table-game players who can't afford the higher stakes at today's table games or don't want to play the table games anymore. Video-poker players, especially the younger ones, tend to be better educated; a substantial minority of them have college degrees or at least some college education. There is no doubt in my mind that if the current video-poker trends continue, video poker will be the dominant casino game in the near future."

Another Las Vegas executive said: "Video poker offers what table games offer but at a lower price. You get to make choices, you get to fully participate in the game. But unlike table games, no one is overlooking your play. No one is second-guessing the choices that you make. It's just you and the machine and only your bankbook knows for sure just how you're doing. Here in Vegas, video poker is a good bet as well. The player knows he is getting a good run for his money. In fact, some video-poker machines pay out more than the table games do if you know the right strategies."

It would not be a stretch of the imagination to postulate that the growth in video-poker play is a direct result of the aging of the video-games generation of the 1970s. The donkey-kongsters of the 1970s have become the video-poker aficionados of today's expanding casino empire. These are people who cut their teeth on the video screen and now have gone on to bigger and better video experiences. As kids their egos and neighborhood reputations were on the line in their video games—now it's their money. What a rush! And their numbers will continue to balloon as each succeeding generation of video-gamesters comes into its maturity. In the future we might see on-line video machines directly linked to casinos where a player can build up credits and debits on some type of credit card—in the privacy and convenience of his own home.

Dr. Marvin Karlins, psychologist, gaming expert, and author of many works both in and out of the gaming field, including the seminal *Psyching Out Las Vegas!*, addressed this very issue when I spoke to him regarding the phenomenal growth of machine play in today's casinos. "Today's video-poker machines offer the players a good gamble for their money. With the proper strategies on some machines the players can even have a slight edge over the casino. For a gambler it doesn't get any better than that. It also affords the player two very important psychological inducements for playing—anonymity and autonomy—in addition to the possibility of winning some money. There are choices to make but no one to criticize you if you seemingly make the wrong choice. This would especially appeal to people who are somewhat anxious with the thought of approaching table games where you would have to interact with many others—some of whom might be critical of your play."

So we can use simple addition to figure out why video poker is the growth game in casinoland. Video generation + choice + good gamble + reasonable betting limits + no one bothering you = growth of video poker.

In the words of one former casino executive who now spends his leisure playing video Jacks-or-Better Draw Poker: "I envision the casinos of 30 or 40 years from now as fundamentally different places than the casinos of today. The table-game area will be pushed into some small corner of the casino and will be dominated by blackjack. There will be one or two craps tables and several roulette wheels off to the side and that's about it. But the table-game area will be an afterthought just like the slot-machine areas were afterthoughts in the 1950s. The rest of the casino will consist of acres and acres of machines—most of them video poker. Some of them will be games that we haven't yet invented but will appeal to the generations brought up on combat video games like Mortal Kombat and such. The only noise will be machine sounds and the occasional shout of the jackpot winners. The casino gambler of 30 years ago, like the human being of a thousand years ago, would not recognize except in a vague way the casino of the future—it will be that different."

And why did he play video poker? As a casino executive, hadn't he seen nothing but losers over the years? "That's where video poker differs from most games. In Nevada you can play machines that have only a slight casino edge or are break-even propositions or, in some cases, there are machines that a player can actually beat in the long run. If you enjoy gambling, these machines are good bets. You aren't really risking all that much and you are getting hours and hours of entertainment value for your hard-earned dollar."

Walk down any video-poker aisle and you will see a number of video-generation players, those twenty-or-thirty-somethings, challenging the gods of chance as they once challenged Pac-Man. For them video poker is just another form of interactive games-playing. Unfortunately, most of them get eaten alive, or rather their bankrolls do, since they are playing inferior machines with poor paybacks, or they are playing strategies that even on the best machines will incur long-term losses. Sadly, some may even be playing machines that only appear to be video-poker machines but are in actuality "slot machines in video-poker machines' clothing" as I reveal in Chapter 12. On these machines even expert play will result in long-term losses because the machines are *legally* rigged—to put it bluntly.

With all that said—here's a marvelous fact: *video poker can be beaten*. It can be beaten in the short run by luck, of course—and anyone, be he a fool or a philosopher, can be visited by Dame Fortune on occasion. But, more importantly, video poker can be beaten in the long run by using the proper strategies. If—isn't there always an "if" in life?—*if* you play these good strategies on good machines. What are good machines? Machines that return close to, at, or over 100 percent of the money put in them.

Unlike real life, which is a negative expectation game since it always ends in the death of the player (you and me, unfortunately), some video-poker machines are positive expectation devices. In the long run our bankrolls can grow and prosper. But not all casino video games can offer us the hope of long-run gains. While video craps has a marvelous payout percentage compared to most regular slots (proper play = a 98.6 percent payback), it still is a negative expectation game. Video keno is a loser with house edges in the double digits—just like its table-game kinsman.

Video poker and its cousin video blackjack have as their underpinnings a delightful mixture of chance and design. The game is dealt randomly from a deck of cards (usually 52, sometimes 53 or more in some wild-card video-poker games) and those cards will fall as they may. However, once the initial hand is dealt, fate must take a back seat to free will because the player is now in control. His choices, his strategy and money management methods, his knowledge of play will ultimately determine his future earnings.

There is only one caveat, as I've mentioned, and that is this: you have to select the right machines to play. This book will steer you to those machines and give you the proper strategies to attain victory. But the choice of playing them is up to you.

The Continuum of Freedom

Let us take a look at the machine games in a somewhat different light. If I use my fate vs. free will analogy, we can place the machine games on a continuum—from left to right according to the amount of choice offered the player. The fact that a machine is under "free will" does not necessarily mean that all machines of this type will offer the same games. Some video-poker and video-blackjack games are decidedly inferior in terms of their paybacks (even for expert play) than are some slot machines. But all things being equal, the best video-poker and video-blackjack games are better than the best slot machines because they offer a better than 100 percent return and this return is fundamentally a product of the player's skill in choosing which hands to play and how to play them.

FATE	LIMITED FREE WILL	FREE WILL
Slot machines	Video keno	Video blackjack
	Video craps	Video poker

The slot machine offers only a limited number of choices, as previously discussed. You get to pick your machine and decide for how long and for how much you'll play. But once the coin is deposited, the god-in-the-machine takes over and merely informs you of your fate. Range of paybacks vary— from very good (99 percent) to poor (80 percent or lower), depending on where you play.

In video keno, you get to pick the machine and decide for how much and for how long you'll play. But you also get to choose which numbers are yours. Then the god-in-the-machine picks its numbers. You learn your fate. On every turn you can bet more or less, fewer or greater total numbers. Payback is poor (75 percent).

In video craps, you get to pick the machine and decide for how much and for how long to play. You also get to select which bets to try and which to avoid. When the shooter-in-the-machine rolls, you await the decision. Range of paybacks are from very good (98.6) to poor (83 percent).

In video blackjack you get to select the machine and know whether it's a good machine or a poor machine based on the payout scale and rules. You decide how to play the cards dealt you. Card counting can give you an edge on some machines. Skill is the determining factor in the long run for good players. Payout range for expert play is excellent (100+ percent) to fair (98 percent).

Video poker has the same skill factor as video blackjack but the player has a multitude of machines and types of games to choose from. Blackjack is essentially blackjack. But video poker comes in an amazing assortment of games—each with its own distinct strategies. You can determine which games are worth playing and which should be avoided. You can determine how much to play for. Expert play is the deciding factor in the long run. Payout range is excellent (100+ percent) to poor (80 percent).

So pick the right machines, play them properly and you can wrest victory at video poker and video blackjack!

Now, let's get it on.

2

Programming, Percentages, Probabilities, Procedures and Your Psyche

I.
The Dealer in the Machine

Sitting inside every video-poker or video-blackjack machine is a dealer. Just as in any card game played in a casino, the dealer shuffles the cards, deals the cards, collects the discards and determines who gets paid when the hand is completed. The dealer is (or should be) uninterested in who wins or loses, as his job is only to shuffle and deal and collect those cards—and keep the game moving.

However, the dealer-in-the-machine is of a very special and particular kind that sets him far apart from his human counterpart in the casino poker rooms. The dealer-in-the-machine never gets tired. Also, he rarely makes a mistake. When he senses that he isn't up to par, he can shut himself down and signal for help. That's because the

dealer-in-the-machine is a microchip that has been programmed to select a series of random numbers. These numbers correspond to the various cards being used and the
sequences of numbers will correspond to various hands that
will be dealt. In games that are not rigged, the cards will be
shuffled at random and dealt as they come off the top of the
deck. Thus, the first number sequence will be the first card, the
second number sequence will be the second card and so forth.
Just as a human dealer would do. In theory and sans cheating,
each card will have the same chance of coming up as every
other card in the deck or as every other card in the remaining
portion of the deck.

Another interesting difference between a human dealer
and the dealer-in-the-machine is the fact that the dealer-in-the-
machine is constantly selecting number sequences—even when
the machine isn't being played! In this frenetic solitaire, the
dealer-in-the-machine is selecting, arranging, and discarding,
selecting, arranging, and discarding numbers upon numbers,
sequences upon sequences, cards after cards, hands after
hands, as he waits for some player to ante up.

Once the player antes up—that is, puts his coins in the
machine—the dealer-in-the-machine signals the video-display
portion of the device that thus and such cards will come up in
this and that order. And the game is on. The player will now
make his choices of keeping or drawing some cards, all cards or
no cards. The player does this by pushing the DEAL-DRAW
button on the console.

II.
Serial Dealing or Parallel Dealing?

The majority of video-poker machines in the past had parallel dealing. A parallel machine is one where the cards are
dealt with their replacements already selected and in place
"behind" the displayed card. Thus, if you received a card that
you didn't want and discarded it, the card that replaced it
would have been sitting there all along. In a real card game,

the replacement card would not have already been dealt. Instead, the replacements are made in the order of discard and off the top of the deck. The first card discarded would receive the first card off the top of the deck, the second card discarded would receive the second card off the top of the deck and so forth until all discards had been replaced with new cards. Some of the newer machines employ this kind of serial dealing—just as a regular card game would. In either case, if the game is dealt fairly and the microchip isn't programmed to avoid certain hands, the video-poker player can be confident in employing the strategies discussed in this book for the machine he selects to play. The type of deal has little impact on the long-range prospects of the skillful player.

III.
The Difference between Video-Poker Machines and Slot Machines

In reality, video-poker machines are slot machines but they are slot machines of a very special sort. Like regular slots, the random-number generator (or dealer-in-the-machine) selects the sequences at random and these sequences correspond to the symbols that will be displayed for the players. In the case of video poker, these sequences or symbols will be displayed by card values. However, unlike regular slot machines, the video-poker machine is easily readable and the player can determine exactly what the percentage payback is on the type of machine he wishes to play. The video-poker player can ascertain if he is playing a machine that pays 96 percent of all the money put in it, or 98 percent, or even a hundred percent or more. The slot player has no such knowledge. He doesn't know whether he's playing a 99 percent return machine or an 83 percent return machine because these values are hidden in the programming of the machine. There is no method in slots for analyzing the type of machine you are playing vis-à-vis the casino edge.

Not so with a video-poker machine. Assuming honesty in programming, the video-poker player knows exactly what the odds are that he faces for any given hand, since these odds are based on a 52-card deck or, in the case of games with jokers, decks of 53 or more cards. The video-poker player also knows exactly what percentage edge the casino has over him or what edge he has over the casino since this can be determined by analyzing the payoff schedule printed prominently on the face of the machine. The casino's or player's edge is determined by the amount of the payoffs for the various hands—always assuming that the player is using the correct strategies for the machine he is playing and that the machine is dealing an honest game.

This is a radical departure from traditional slots where most everything is a great unknown. Yes, the slot player knows that if he lines up certain symbols, he'll be paid a certain amount of money, but what he doesn't know is the frequency of these symbols' appearance. Without such knowledge the slot player cannot determine the nature of the risk he is taking when playing any given machine. Thankfully, slot players can now make a strong, educated guess as to which machines are loose and which are tight by using the revelations made in my book *Break the One-Armed Bandits!* concerning their placement in the casino. In addition, slot players have an excellent chance of finding and distinguishing which of several machines would be loose or tight in relation to each other by following the advice I gave in my newsletter *Chance and Circumstance* ("Slot Revelation: Using the Casinos' Computers Against Them," $15, Paone Press, Box 610, Lynbrook, NY 11563). Still the most astute slot player cannot know with certainty the *exact* percentages he faces on all machines and kinds of games as can a video-poker player. The slot player must resort to cleverness and outside information to ferret out good machines. The video-poker player merely has to understand how to read the machine's chart.

Thus, there is no secret to which video-poker machines are "loose" and which are "tight" as there is with traditional slots. That's because the loose and tight machines can be distinguished rather easily. With the proper playing strategies, the loose machines can be beaten by the player. Naturally, the tight machines far outweigh the loose ones in the land of video poker, but that's the way of it in the casino world. The casinos are not in the business of making it easy for the patron to win. Their mission is to make it easy for you to lose and even easier for you to actually enjoy losing. Luckily, the astute player doesn't have to join the chorus in this choir of the lost because he can select his machines carefully and be confident that he has a damn good shot at the casino's money. In video poker the player can get the best of it. Indeed, in Nevada you will find a great many machines that are worth playing and it's a dollar-wise but pound-foolish player who selects video poker as his game and then doesn't play the best machines and the best strategies.

IV.
Video Poker vs. Poker Poker

Although video poker and regular poker share much of the same terminology and many of the same concepts, they are radically different games. In poker you are competing against other players and even strong hands can lose if the player playing those hands is weak or if someone else has a better hand. Likewise, a player with a garbage hand can bluff his opponents into submission and steal the pot. Poker is a game that combines psychology, probability, and luck. It's the gambling equivalent of real mortal combat. Now, while psychology certainly plays a part in all forms of gambling, in poker you are as concerned with your opponents' psychology as you are with your own. True, you must know yourself, but it is just as important to know your opponents.

On the other hand, video poker is a game played against the probabilities programmed in a machine. A good hand in video poker always wins whatever the stipulated amount is. You can't be beaten by a better hand. (Okay, a player could conceivably discard a good hand by accident and wind up a loser.) You are not playing against other players. You are not in a battle of wills and cunning with your fellow human beings. There is no trickery, no combat psychology, no human interaction. The winning combinations are set in stone, so to speak. You can't bluff or con a machine.

But still—you can beat that machine.

In that sense your psychology certainly does play a part. To beat the video-poker machine, you must be prepared to play only the very best strategies and these only on the very best machines. You must prepare yourself for the streaky nature of video poker. There are l-o-n-g s-t-r-e-t-c-h-e-s where you will lose and lose and lose—even on the very best machines and with the very best strategies. In fact, in all likelihood you will lose more sessions at video poker than you will win because that is the nature of the game.

The above bears repeating, so write it on the tablets of your heart: *you will lose more sessions than you will win because that is the nature of the game.* You have to be psychologically prepared for this. Video poker is a game of DOWNS and UPS. More DOWNS. Fewer UPS. But on the right machines, that is, 100 percent or more payback machines, and in the long run, your "fewer UPS" will generate much more income than your "more DOWNS" will lose and thus you'll come out ahead.

This phenomenon is caused by the fact that the jackpot for a royal flush must be factored into the percentages of a machine for determining its playability. A natural royal flush (no wild cards or jokers) occurs approximately once in every 40,000 hands if we use the Jacks or Better machine as the model. It's usually a long time coming. But when it comes, it can push the player from the red into the black. Of course, just because the probability of a natural royal flush is a one-in-40,000 chance doesn't mean that it will necessarily come up that way in the real world. Chance itself is streaky and events sometimes bunch up or elongate. It's unpredictable. You might hit a lucky streak where you get several natural royals in several hundred or thousand hands. You also might hit a cold streak where you play for years and years, hundreds of thousands of hands, and don't get a single one. I know people who seem to have gotten an unbelievable share of royals in the past two years. I also know people who have not gotten a single one. The latter situation can be disheartening to say the least.

Of course, no number of natural royal flushes can make you a theoretical long-term winner on negative-expectation machines. If the machine is returning less than 100 percent, then you can expect in the long run to lose whatever percentage hold that machine has. However, machines that range from 99 percent payback to 99.9 percent payback can be beaten if you factor in comps for your play. The little you lose can be more than made up by the perks the casino is willing to give you for your play.

Again, in the real world even negative-expectation devices do have some lucky players. You'll meet one such player in Chapter Twelve who has hit so many jackpots and received so many comps from Atlantic City casinos that she will be hard pressed to give it all back. This despite the fact that she plays mostly negative-expectation machines (or worse, rigged machines!). The real world and the world of theory sometimes diverge.

V.
The Ranking of Hands and Types of Draws

Video-poker hands are ranked the same way as hands in regular poker. The following list of hands is from the highest ranking to the lowest ranking.

Royal Flush: 10, jack, queen, king, ace of the same suit.

Straight Flush: Any five cards of the same suit in sequence. Example: three, four, five, six, and seven of diamonds.

Four of a Kind: Four cards of the same type. Example: four nines.

Full House: Three of a kind and two of a kind. Example: three jacks, two aces.

Flush: Any five cards of the same suit not in sequence. Example: two, four, eight, nine and ace of spades.

Straight: Five cards in sequence not of the same suit. Example: eight of hearts, nine of clubs, ten of diamonds, jack of spades, queen of spades.

Three of a Kind: Three cards of the same rank. Example: three aces.

Two Pair: Two cards of one rank and two cards of another rank. Example: two tens and two queens.

One Pair: Two cards of the same rank. Example: two nines.

High Card: The order of ranking for the cards from highest to lowest is: ace, king, queen, jack, ten, nine, eight, seven, six, five, four, three, two, one.

Once you know the ranking of the hands, you should be familiar with the types of draws you can make. Other than discarding cards in order to draw to a pair, two pairs, three-of-a-kind, or a flush, you will be drawing to various straights and straight flushes. These types of hands come in two categories, those that require an *inside* draw and those require an *outside* draw. If you have four cards to the following straight—eight, nine, jack, queen, and two—you would discard the two and draw to the other four, hoping to get the ten. This is an inside draw because the card you need fits inside the sequence. An outside draw would occur when you have nine, ten, jack, queen and two. You would discard the two and hope for one card to fit either *outside* end of the sequence. Sometimes this is referred to as an *open* draw because the ends of the draw are open. (Gambling terminology is nothing if not logical!) Thus, if you have an open-ended straight it means that either end is open for a card. Likewise a *double-inside draw* would be an attempt to draw two inside cards to make a straight or a straight flush. When you are looking over the strategies in the upcoming chapters be aware that straights and flushes are often divided up based on how many inside draws are needed. If the strategy doesn't specify any particular inside or outside draw, you can assume that either is the preferred strategy. Thus, you would draw to the straight or straight flush whether it's an outside or an inside one.

What every video-poker player hopes for are the "no-brainer" hands that are automatic winners. These are hands that don't require any decision making on the part of the player because they are rarely broken up. The following is a list of such "pat" hands. If you receive them on your first five cards, simply keep all your cards by hitting the HOLD button and then the DEAL-DRAW button.

However, sometimes even pat hands have to be broken in order to go for the money. Thus, in the strategies that follow I will note on what occasions you should break a pat hand. In general such an eventuality occurs when you have four cards to a royal flush with a fifth card of the same suit (a flush) or you have a straight made with a fifth card not of the same suit. Despite the fact that you have a winner, you would discard the "fifth" card and go for the better hand.

But first, the ranking of the "pat hands" is as follows:

Royal Flush

Straight Flush

Four of a Kind

Full House

Flush

Straight

VI.
Video Poker Procedures

A slot machine is simple. You place your coins in and either push a button or pull a handle. The reels spin and a decision is rendered. Then you repeat the procedure. However, video poker is somewhat more complicated because the player interacts with the machine and where there's human choice, there can be human mistakes. So a wise player should know the mechanics of play as well as the strategies for play. You want to play in a smooth, swift, yet unhurried and unharried manner. Your mechanics should be perfect because a mistake could cost you money.

Step One: You put your coin or coins in. If you are playing full coin, then the machine will automatically deal you your initial hand. However, if you are playing less than full coin, you must hit the DEAL-DRAW button for the machine to deal the initial hand.

Step Two: You now analyze your hand. You will have to make one of the following choices: A.) Keep all the cards because you have a pat hand, or b.) discard all the cards because you have garbage, or c.) discard some cards and keep others.

To keep all the cards, you press the HOLD button under each card. Then you hit the DEAL-DRAW button. Since nothing is being dealt, the machine will record your win and either pay you or give you CREDITS.

To discard all cards, you simply hit the DEAL-DRAW button and all the cards will be replaced with new cards. If your new hand is a winner, the machine will record your win and either pay you or give you CREDITS.

To discard some cards and keep others, you press the HOLD button under the cards you wish to keep and then press DEAL-DRAW to replace the cards you wish to get rid of. These cards will be replaced and the machine will record your win (if you won) and either pay you or give you CREDITS. The key to success at video poker is to know what cards to hold and what cards to throw away.

Cautions: Make sure that when you hold a card that the word HELD lights up under the card. Sometimes the machine doesn't register your press of the HOLD button—for whatever reason. So you'll just have to press it again. Otherwise you'll discard the card when you hit DEAL-DRAW. If you do get a pat hand, do not think the machine registers it automatically. It doesn't. You must press HOLD for each card. Imagine getting a full house, four of a kind, a straight flush or, God forbid, a royal flush only to forget to hit HOLD for each card... frightening thought. But it does happen. I heard one story where a husband and wife were playing together at the Mirage in Las Vegas. The wife hit a wild-card royal and the husband was so excited that before she could hit the HOLD button under each card, he had reached over and hit DEAL-DRAW. The wild-card royal vanished to be replaced with nothing. The wife paused slightly to digest the happening, turned to her husband, who was described by the security guard as "a big, strapping guy," and slugged him right in the mouth.

So the mechanics of your play must include checking to

see if the HELD sign lights up under the cards you are keeping before you hit the DEAL-DRAW button—either that or have a very forgiving wife.

Also, if you are playing coins and saving up credits, make sure you actually *cash out your credits before you go*. I know of cases where people didn't do this and left the machine thinking they hadn't won anything. This can happen because most video-poker machines automatically record your win as a CREDIT and you must press the CASH OUT button for the money to fall into the tray. I benefited from this recently at the Rio in Las Vegas. I went to a machine and as I was putting my coins in, I noticed that the credit light was flashing. I looked at the screen and there were 20 coins in credit on that machine. The person who had played the machine before me had evidently left, leaving behind a win for me. From my observations, the majority of people who leave their credits in the machine tend to be casual players who have just put a few coins in and then don't realize they have won. Often these people are strollers, ambling through the slot aisles, putting in coins and then not taking their credits. Of course, their loss can be someone else's gain.

In Vegas there's a man known as "Rat Tails," so dubbed because of his greasy hair that hangs, well, like rat tails over his shoulders. He also has a somewhat bug-eyed look. His appearance is rather reminiscent of the Pardoner's from Chaucer's *Canterbury Tales*. He usually works downtown where his unkempt appearance doesn't look so out of place. Occasionally, he can be found on the Strip. He is not a thief, for what he does is not illegal. He is a roamer. And scavenger. He roams the slot aisles looking for machines whose CREDITS have not been cashed out, or whose trays have a few coins that have been overlooked by patrons. He also checks the floors for coins, "particularly those lush places where the coins blend into the carpeting." This is how he makes his daily bread—or, rather, daily bottle—for he frequents his own version of "lush places" to spend his hard-found coin.

"I find a lot of quarters left behind," he says. "Sometimes you find dollar coins but mostly it's quarters. The quarters sometimes are sitting up against the wall of the tray and the person missed it when he took his coins. I find credits too, usually late at night on the weekends when people have had a little too much to drink. On the floor too. You'd be surprised how much money is just sitting on the casino floor. So I always walk with my head down."

He claims he makes "anywhere from $20 on weekdays to $100 a day on weekends." However, it isn't all fun for Mr. Rat Tails. "I work a full day mostly. I think of it as a job. I can probably tell you what kind of carpet is in what casino. If they had a game show like *Match the Carpet to the Casino,* I'd be a winner."

Is the finding of credits or coins in trays or on the floor so unusual? One security guard at Caesars Palace told me that on a weekend night "you could walk from one end of the casino to the other and probably find $50 worth of coins on the carpet. Then come back in a couple of hours and find $50 more."

So keep a close tab on your CREDITS and your coins.

Another caution is in order here as well. Many books and articles on video poker extol the virtue of speed in the playing of video-poker hands—on full-payback machines, that is. Since the player has a long-term edge (or an even game) which will materialize over time, the more hands played, the better the chances for a royal flush and ultimate victory. While this is theoretically true, the old adage that "haste makes waste" applies to video poker. You want to play with speed, certainly. But there's a difference between playing smoothly and with speed and playing hurriedly. The latter will inevitably lead to mistakes that you can ill afford to make; mistakes that will, in the long run, lead to a diminishing of your edge. Just as a good golfer or tennis player concerns himself with the mechanics of his game, so too must a good video-poker player. If a slight reduction in your speed simultaneously reduces your frequency of mistakes, then you are helping yourself in the long run. In video poker speed sometimes kills.

VI.
Types of Video-Poker Games

You are now entering an Alice-in-Wonderland world where, to quote Macbeth, "nothing is but what is not." Not all video-poker games are created equal. Even games with the same names on identical-looking machines are not necessarily the same game calling for the same strategies because the payout scale is different. *The key variable in video poker of any type is the payout scale.* For example, there are more than 20 varieties of Joker Wild Poker (Joker Poker) machines in operation. Yet, a close look at their payout scales shows that all are different in terms of the house's edge over the player—even if they appear to be the identical Joker Wild Game (for example: Joker Wild Jacks or Better). These payback percentages range from 102 percent (the player will get back $1.02 for every dollar put in the machine in the long run) to 88 percent (the player will get 88 cents back for every dollar put in the machine)—and this assumes that the player plays a perfect strategy for that machine. That's some big difference. You have to play perfectly to get back 88 percent? Yuck!

And the same holds true on the myriad machines and versions of machines throughout the video-poker world.

Indeed, at present count, over one hundred different video-poker games can be currently found on the floors of America's and the world's casinos. Many of these are variations of the following types: *Jacks or Better Draw Poker, Tens or Better Draw Poker, Deuces Wild Poker, Joker Wild Poker (Joker Poker),* and *Deuces and Joker Wild Poker.* Sometimes machines can be found that have bonus hands, second chance options and the like. To offer such options, the pay scale for the other hands has to be downgraded; more often than not such downgrading will totally eliminate the player's previous edge on this type of machine. Be doubly cautious because machines with the *exact* same names (say, All-American Draw Poker) can offer different payouts. You must read the payout schedule to know if a rose by the same name is a sweet-smelling flower or a horrible stinkweed. In video poker, what's in a name? Very little. It's the numbers that count. So pay attention to the payout scale.

It is also important to understand how to read a payout scale properly.

If we take the typical full-pay Jacks or Better, five-coin maximum machine, the payout will look like this:

Hand	1 coin	2 coin	3 coin	4 coin	5 coin
Royal Flush	250	500	750	1000	4700
Straight Flush	50	100	150	200	250
Four of a Kind	25	50	75	100	125
Full House	9	18	27	36	45
Flush	6	12	18	24	30
Straight	4	8	12	16	20
Three of a Kind	3	6	9	12	15
Two Pairs	2	4	6	8	10
Jacks or better	1	2	3	4	5

However, we are not interested in playing this machine or any video-poker machine for less than full coin, so we are only interested in the five-coin line. Here we see that all the five-coin hands are merely multiples of the first line (i.e., the full house is nine coins on line one and five times that on line five, 45 coins) except for the royal flush line, which is 4,700 coins. The shorthand we will use in this book, therefore, is to divide the royal flush (or any special bonus hand) by whatever the total maximum coin is (in this case five) to arrive at a payscale that can be easily read. So, my description of the above machine will read as follows:

Jacks or Better Draw Poker
9/6 Machine with 4,700 coins
for Royal Flush
99.85 % Payback

Royal Flush 940
Straight Flush 50
Four of a Kind 25
Full House 9
Flush 6
Straight 4
Three of a Kind 3
Two Pairs 2
Pair of Jacks or better 1

You will note that we have simply divided the 4,700 coin payout of the royal flush on the fifth line by five, getting 940. The other lines reflect their line one payouts since these stay proportionally the same on the all-important line five. This is the common construction for describing video-poker machines. For those of you who wish to read other books on the topic (see "Recommended Reading" in the appendix), you will find that most video-poker authors use it in describing machines.

Still, with over a hundred varieties of video poker to choose from, what is the weary though wary player to do?

It's relatively easy, really.

Pick the best version of the game you enjoy playing and *stick to playing that version of that game*. Forget all the rest. Become an expert in that one version of the game. Do this and you can not only have your game but beat it too. If playing one game is not to your liking then select the best versions of two or three games and play exclusively on those. This in and of itself is the most important factor for the video-poker player. Do not become lost in the jungle of options that the casinos plant before you. Most of the games aren't worth playing. However, for most locations in the country, you will be able to find some wheat sprinkled amongst the chaff to make your video-poker playing experience enjoyable and rewarding.

While you, as a player, face the task of deciding which video-poker games to play, I, as a writer, have to decide which video-poker games to analyze and offer strategies for. Would I be doing anyone a service by offering the correct strategy for playing a machine that returns 88 percent when right next to it will be a machine of the same general type paying 99 percent or more? Who are my readers anyway? The fact that you are reading this book is prima facie evidence that you desire to win. You obviously aren't one of the hordes who wander through the casinos and plop yourself down at any machine on a whim and a prayer. So why should I waste my time and your time with strategies for machines you or I wouldn't (or shouldn't) be caught dead playing?

So I won't.

What I shall do is this: I'll offer solid strategies for the best-paying machines of the various games. For the poorer versions of these games, I will alert you to the percentages you face should you decide (sadly) to play these versions. I'll take a rather arbitrary definition of "best machine" and postulate that any machine version of video poker that returns 98% or more is a good bet. These will be my "Group A" machines. "Group B" will be machines that you can play if none of the "Group A" machines are available in your area. The percentages for "Group B" machines will range between 95% and 97.9%. "Group C" are machines that I don't recommend, machines that fall under 94.9% percent return, but I'll alert you to their paybacks so you will be able to recognize them and avoid them. Next, I shall spend some time on proper money-management techniques, bankroll requirements and mental preparation.

Remember: I want you to have victory at video poker and to do this you have to know which battles are worth fighting and which you should retreat from.

3

Victory at Jacks-or-Better Draw Video Poker

It's the granddaddy of all the video-poker games and, in the estimation of many players and experts alike, Jacks-or-Better video poker is still the best and brightest game to play if you want to have a shot at long-term wins. The best Jacks-or-Better machines return between 99.5 and 99.85 percent and some even go over the 100 percent payback threshold. The game is also attractive because it is not quite as volatile as the other forms of video poker. Volatility in video-poker terminology just means long stretches of losing punctuated by explosive winning sessions. Jacks-or-Better is a little smoother than these other varieties. Of course, like all video-poker machines, you will experience more losing sessions than winning sessions since you must factor in that 40,000-to-one royal flush in determining the payback percentage.

My personal experience, for what it's worth, indicates that on the days when I've received one or more four-of-a-kind hands, those were my winning days. So four-of-a-kind has become a bellwether for me, and in Jacks-or-Better you can expect four-of-a kind to appear approximately once every 425 hands. If we assume a four-hour playing day (divided up into any number of sessions you want), with one hand every 20 seconds or so, you can expect to play in the vicinity of 720 hands. It would not be unusual to receive one, two or three four-of-a-kinds in that number of hands. (It also wouldn't be unheard of to receive none.)

Percentages of Jacks or Better

The percentages that follow are based on perfect playing of the strategies in this book for the best type of Jacks-or-Better machines. If I say that the four of a kind is a 424-to-one shot, it will be a much greater long shot if the player decides to discard every three-of-a-kind hand he receives on the initial round. In addition, each version of Jacks-or-Better video poker that is less than a full-pay machine has slightly different percentages because some of the strategies for these machines are different and—it bears repeating—strategies alter the percentages. However, the following percentages are merely to give you an idea of what to expect—in general. So consider the following figures as close approximations. You will note that the full house is an easier hand to make than either the flush or the straight, yet it is paid more. Go figure.

```
Royal Flush . . . . . . . . . . . . . . . . . 40,399 to 1
Straight Flush . . . . . . . . . . . . . . . . 9,199 to 1
Four of a Kind . . . . . . . . . . . . . . . . 424 to 1
Full House . . . . . . . . . . . . . . . . . . 86 to 1
Flush . . . . . . . . . . . . . . . . . . . . . 90 to 1
Straight . . . . . . . . . . . . . . . . . . . 88 to 1
Three of a Kind . . . . . . . . . . . . . . . 13 to 1
Two Pairs . . . . . . . . . . . . . . . . . . . 7 to 1
Pair of Jacks or better . . . . . . . . . . . . 4 to 1
(Approximately 55% of all hands are losers.)
```

Group A:

The Machines You Should Play
98% to 100+% Paybacks

(Remember all the tables reflect per coin on five-coin play. Your original bet is considered part of the return as well. All the following machines pay back at least 98% of the money put in them—for expert play.)

Jacks or Better Draw Poker 9/6 Machine with 5,000 coins for Royal Flush 100% Payback*

Royal Flush 1,000**
Straight Flush 50
Four of a Kind 25
Full House 9
Flush 6
Straight 4
Three of a Kind 3
Two Pairs 2
Pair of Jacks or better 1

Jacks or Better Draw Poker 9/6 Machine with 4,700 coins for Royal Flush 99.85% Payback*

Royal Flush 940**
Straight Flush 50
Four of a Kind 25
Full House 9
Flush 6

Straight 4
Three of a Kind 3
Two Pairs 2
Pair of Jacks or better 1

9/6* Machine with 4,000 coins for Royal Flush 99.5% Payback

Royal Flush 800**
Straight Flush 50
Four of a Kind 25
Full House 9
Flush 6
Straight 4
Three of a Kind 3
Two Pairs 2
Pair of Jacks or better 1

*Jacks or Better Machines are often catalogued by their payouts on the Full House and Flush lines, since these are often the lines that are altered to increase or decrease the house edge. Thus, a 9/6 machine is a machine that returns nine coins on the Full House and six coins on the Flush.

** Minimum progressive jackpots necessary for 100%+ paybacks are as follows: Nickels—$251; Quarters—$1,252; Dollars—$5,002.

Strategy for 9/6 Jacks or Better

The way to look at strategy for Jacks-or-Better video poker (and by extension all video poker) is to list the hands in order of priority. The hands on top should always be played regardless of what you have to break up to play them. Thus, if you had a low pair and a four-card straight with one high card, you would keep the low pair and discard all the rest because in the long run you will make more money by keeping that low pair. Or, if you had four to a flush but three of those are to a royal flush, you would go for the royal flush.

1. All pat hands….stand.

2. Four cards to a royal flush…draw one card (break anything else including a flush or straight)

3. Three of a kind…draw two cards

4. Four cards to a straight flush—open ended…draw one card (break anything else)

5. Two pairs…draw one card

6. Four cards to straight flush—inside draw…draw one card (break anything else)

7. Pair of jacks or better…draw three cards (break anything except hands above)

8. Three cards to a royal flush…draw two cards (break anything except hands above)

9. Four cards to a flush…draw one card (break anything except hands above)

10. Four cards to a straight with three high cards—outside draw…draw one card (break anything except hands above)

11. Low pair…draw three cards (break anything except hands above)

12. Four cards to a straight with fewer than three high cards—outside draw …draw one card (break anything except hands above)

13. Three cards to a straight flush…draw two cards (break anything except hands above)

14. Two cards to a royal flush…draw three cards (break anything except hands above)

15. Three cards to a straight flush—inside draws…draw two cards (break anything except hands above)

16. Four cards to a straight with three high cards—inside draw…draw one card (break anything except hands above)

17. One, two or three high cards…draw four, three, or two cards (break anything except hands above)

18. All other hands…draw five cards (break anything except hands above)

Progressive 8/5 Jacks or Better Draw Poker 99.5% to 100+%

(Progressives: Must be at least 8,960 coins—or $448 on nickel machines; $2,240 on quarter machines; $8,960 on dollar machines; $44,800 on five dollar machines—to be worth playing. That's because the payout for the full house and the flush have been reduced to 8 and 5 respectively. Below 8,000 coins you are giving away too much. Above 8,000 coins you have 100% or more return…if you hit that royal.)

Royal Flush . . . . Progressive
Straight Flush 50
Four of a Kind 25
Full House 8
Flush 5
Straight 4
Three of a Kind 3
Two Pairs 2
Pair of Jacks or better 1

Strategy for 8/5 Progressives

1. All pat hands…stand

2. Four cards to a royal flush…draw one card (break anything including a straight or a flush)

3. Three of a kind…draw two cards

4. Four cards to a straight flush—outside draw…draw one card (break anything except hands above)

5. Two pairs…draw one card

6. Four cards to a straight flush—inside draw…draw one card (break anything except hands above)

7. Three cards to a royal flush…draw two cards (break anything except hands above)

8. Jacks or better…draw three cards (break anything except hands above)

9. Four cards to a flush...draw one card *(break anything except hands above)*

10. Four cards to a straight with two or three high cards—outside draw...draw one card *(break anything except hands above)*

11. Low pair...draw three cards *(break anything except hands above)*

12. Four cards to a straight with fewer than two high cards—outside draw...draw one card *(break anything except hands above)*

13. Three cards to a straight flush—inside or outside draws...draw two cards *(break anything except hands above)*

14. Four cards to a straight with ace high—inside draw...draw one card *(break anything except hands above)*

15. Two cards to a royal flush...draw three cards *(break anything except hands above)*

16. One, two, or three high cards...draw four, three, or two cards *(break anything except hands above)*

17. All other hands...discard and draw five cards

Four of a Kind Bonus Jacks or Better Draw Poker with 4,000 Coins for Royal Flush 99.2% Return

Royal Flush	800
Straight Flush	50
Four Aces	80
Four 2's, 3's, 4's	40
Four 5's through Kings	25
Full House	8
Flush	5
Straight	4
Three of a Kind	3
Two Pairs	2
Jacks or better	1

Strategy for Four of a Kind Bonus Jacks or Better Draw Poker

1. All pat hands...stand

2. Four cards to a royal flush...draw one card *(break anything else including a flush or straight)*

3. Three of a kind...draw two cards

4. Four cards to a straight flush...draw one card *(break anything else)*

5. Two pairs...draw one card

6. Four cards to a straight flush—inside draw...draw one card *(break anything else)*

7. Pair of jacks or better...draw three cards *(break anything except hands above)*

8. Three cards to a royal flush...draw two cards *(break anything except hands above)*

9. Four cards to a flush...draw one card *(break anything except hands above)*

10. Four cards to a straight with two or three high cards...draw one card *(break anything except hands above)*

11. Low pair...draw three cards *(break anything except hands above)*

12. Four cards to a straight with fewer than two high cards—outside draw...draw one card *(break anything except hands above)*

13. Three cards to a straight flush—inside or outside draw(s)...draw two cards *(break anything except hands above)*

14. Four cards to a straight with ace—inside draw...draw one card *(break anything except hands above)*

15. Two cards to the royal flush...draw three cards *(break anything except hands above)*

16. One, two or three high cards...draw four, three or two cards *(break anything except hands above)*

17. Four cards to a straight with three high cards—inside draw...draw one card *(break anything except hands above)*

18. Three cards to a straight flush—inside draws...draw two cards *(break anything except hands above)*

19. All other hands...discard and draw five cards

Aces and Faces
Four of a Kind Bonus Jacks or Better Draw Poker with 4,000 Coins for Royal Flush
99.3% Payback

Royal Flush 800
Straight Flush 50
Four Aces 80
Four Jacks, Queens, Kings 40
Four 2's through 10's 25
Full House 8
Flush 5
Straight 4
Three of a Kind 3
Two Pairs 2
Jacks or better 1

Strategy for Aces and Faces

1. All pat hands...stand

2. Four cards to a royal flush...draw one card *(break anything else including a flush or straight)*

3. Three of a kind...draw two cards

4. Four cards to a straight flush...draw one card *(break anything else)*

5. Two pairs...draw one card

6. Four cards to a straight flush—inside draw...draw one card *(break anything else)*

7. Pair of jacks or better...draw three cards *(break anything except hands above)*

8. Three cards to a royal flush...draw two cards *(break anything except hands above)*

9. Four cards to a flush...draw one card *(break anything except hands above)*

10. Four cards to a straight with two or three high cards—outside draw...draw one card *(break anything except hands above)*

11. Low pairs...draw three cards *(break anything except hands above)*

12. Four cards to a straight with fewer than two high cards—outside draw...draw one card *(break anything except hands above)*

13. Three cards to a straight flush—inside or outside draw(s) ...draw two cards *(break anything except hands above)*

14. Four cards to a straight with ace or three high cards—inside draw...draw one card *(break anything except hands above)*

15. Two cards to the royal flush...draw three cards *(break anything except hands above)*

16. One, two or three high cards...draw four, three or two cards *(break anything except hands above)*

17. Three cards to a straight flush with one high card—inside draws...draw three cards *(break anything except hands above)*

18. All other hands...discard and draw five cards

Aces and Eights
Progressive-Bonus Four of a Kind
Jacks or Better Draw Poker with
4,000 Coins for Royal Flush Bonus on
Sequential Royal—10,000 coins
99.5% to 100% or more Payback

```
Royal Flush . . . . . . . . . . . . . . . . . . . . . . . . 800
Straight Flush . . . . . . . . . . . . . . . . . . . . . . 50
Four Aces . . . . . . . . . . . . . . . . . . . . . . . . . 80*
Four Eights . . . . . . . . . . . . . . . . . . . . . . . . 80*
Four Sevens . . . . . . . . . . . . . . . . . . . . . . . 50
Four of a Kind  . . . . . . . . . . . . . . . . . . . . . 25
Full House  . . . . . . . . . . . . . . . . . . . . . . . . 8
Flush . . . . . . . . . . . . . . . . . . . . . . . . . . . . 5
Straight . . . . . . . . . . . . . . . . . . . . . . . . . . 4
Three of a Kind  . . . . . . . . . . . . . . . . . . . . 3
Two Pairs . . . . . . . . . . . . . . . . . . . . . . . . . 2
Jacks or better  . . . . . . . . . . . . . . . . . . . . . 1
```
* Minimum progressive hand.

Strategy for Aces and Eights

1. All pat hands…stand

2. Four cards to a royal flush…draw one card *(break anything else including a flush or straight)*

3. Three of a kind…draw two cards

4. Four cards to a straight flush…draw one card *(break anything else)*

5. Two pairs…draw one card *(break anything else)*

6. Four cards to a straight flush—inside draw…draw one card *(break anything else)*

7. Pair of jacks or better…draw three cards *(break anything except hands above)*

8. Three cards to the royal flush…draw two cards *(break anything except hands above)*

9. Four cards to a flush…draw one card *(break anything except hands above)*

10. Pair of sevens or eights…draw three cards *(break anything except hands above)*

11. Four cards to a straight with two or three high cards—outside draw…draw one card *(break anything except hands above)*

12. Low pair…draw three cards *(break anything except hands above)*

13. Four cards to a straight with fewer than two high cards—outside draw…draw one card *(break anything except hands above)*

14. Three cards to a straight flush—inside or outside draws …draw two cards *(break anything except hands above)*

15. Four cards to a straight with ace high—inside draw …draw one card *(break anything except hands above)*

16. Two cards to the royal flush…draw three cards *(break anything except hands above)*

17. One, two, or three high cards…draw four, three or two cards *(break anything except hands above)*

18. Four cards to a straight with three high cards—inside draw…draw one card *(break anything except hands above)*

19. Three cards to a straight flush—inside draw(s)…draw two cards *(break anything except hands above)*

20. All other hands…discard and draw five cards

Aces and Jacks
Four of a Kind Bonus Jacks or Better Draw Poker with 4,000 coins for Royal Flush
99.3% Payback

Royal Flush 800
Straight Flush 50
Four Aces 100
Four Jacks 50
Four of a Kind 25
Full House 8
Flush 5
Straight 4
Three of a Kind 3
Two Pairs 2
Jacks or better 1

Strategy for Aces and Jacks

1. All pat hands…stand

2. Four cards to a royal flush…draw one card *(break anything else including a flush or straight)*

3. Three of a kind…draw two cards

4. Four cards to a straight flush…draw one card *(break anything else)*

5. Two pairs…draw one card

6. Four cards to a straight flush—inside draw…draw one card *(break anything except hands above)*

7. Pair of jacks or better…draw three cards *(break anything except hands above)*

8. Three cards to a royal flush…draw two cards *(break anything except hands above)*

9. Four cards to a flush…draw one card *(break anything except hands above)*

10. Four cards to a straight with two or three high cards—outside draw…draw one card *(break anything except hands above)*

11. Low pairs…draw three cards *(break anything except hands above)*

12. Four cards to a straight with fewer than two high cards—outside draw…draw one card *(break anything except hands above)*

13. Three cards to a straight flush…draw three cards *(break anything except hands above)*

14. Four cards to a straight with ace high—inside draw …draw one card *(break anything except hands above)*

15. Two cards to the royal flush…draw three cards *(break anything except hands above)*

16. One, two or three high cards…draw four, three or two cards *(break anything except hands above)*

17. Four cards to a straight with three high cards—inside draw…draw one card *(break anything except hands above)*

18. Three cards to a straight flush—inside draws…draw two cards *(break anything except hands above)*

19. All other hands…discard and draw five cards

High-Low Royal Flush Jacks or Better Draw Poker with 4,000 coins for Royal Flush and for Low Royal (2-6) Flush 99.1% Payback

Royal Flush 800
Lo-Royal Flush 800
Straight Flush 50
Four of a Kind 40
Full House 6
Flush 5

Straight 4
Three of a Kind 3
Two Pairs 2
Jacks or better 1

Strategy for High-Low Royal Flush

1. All pat hands...stand

2. Four cards to a low royal...draw one card *(break anything else including a flush or straight)*

3. Four cards to a royal flush...draw one card *(break anything else including a flush or straight)*

4. Three of a kind...draw two cards

5. Four cards to a straight flush—inside or outside draw...draw one card *(break anything else)*

6. Two pairs...draw one card

7. Pair of jacks or better...draw three cards *(break anything except hands above)*

8. Three cards to a low royal or a royal flush...draw two cards *(break anything except hands above)*

9. Four cards to a flush...draw one card *(break anything except hands above)*

10. Four cards to a straight with three high cards...draw one card *(break anything except hands above)*

11. Low pair...draw three cards *(break anything except hands above)*

12. Four cards to a straight—outside draw...draw one card *(break anything except hands above)*

13. Three cards to a straight flush...draw two cards *(break anything except hands above)*

14. Two cards to a royal flush...draw three cards *(break anything except hands above)*

15. Four cards to a straight—inside draw...draw one card *(break anything except hands above)*

16. Three cards to a straight flush—double inside draw ...draw two cards *(break anything except hands above)*

17. One, two or three high card…draw four, three or two cards *(break anything except hands above)*

18. Three cards to a straight flush with no high cards—double inside draw…draw two cards *(break anything except hands above)*

19. Two cards to a low royal (4, 5 or 5, 6)…draw three cards *(break anything except hands above)*

20. All other hands…discard and draw five cards

Four Plus Four Bonus Jacks or Better Draw Poker with 4,000 coins for Royal Flush 99.6% Payback

Royal Flush 800
Straight Flush 50
Four Aces 80
Four Kings 60
Four Queens 40
Four of a Kind 20
Full House 8
Flush 6
Straight 4
Three of a Kind 3
Two Pairs 2
Jacks or better 1

Strategy for Four Plus Four

1. All pat hands…stand

2. Four cards to the royal flush…draw one card *(break anything else including a flush or straight)*

3. Three of a kind…draw two cards

4. Four cards to a straight flush…draw one card *(break anything else)*

5. Two pairs…draw one card

6. Four cards to a straight flush—inside draw...draw one card *(break anything except hands above)*

7. Pair of jacks or better...draw three cards *(break anything except hands above)*

8. Four cards to a flush...draw one card *(break anything except hands above)*

9. Four cards to a straight with two or three high cards—inside draw...draw one card *(break anything except hands above)*

10. Low pair...draw three cards *(break anything except hands above)*

11. Four cards to a straight...draw one card *(break anything except hands above)*

12. Three cards to a straight flush...draw two cards *(break anything except hands above)*

13. Two cards to the royal flush...draw three cards *(break anything except hands above)*

14. Four cards to a straight with three high cards—inside draw...draw one card *(break anything except hands above)*

15. One, two or three high cards...draw four, three or two cards *(break anything except hands above)*

16. Three cards to a straight flush—double inside draw ...draw two cards *(break anything except hands above)*

17. All other hands...discard and draw five cards

8/5 Jacks or Better Four of a Kind Bonus Draw Poker with 4,000 coins for Royal Flush 98.3% Payback

Royal Flush	800
Straight Flush	100
Four Aces	50
Four 2's, 3's, 4's	40

Four of a Kind 20
Full House 8
Flush 5
Straight 4
Three of a Kind 3
Two Pairs 2
Jacks or better 1

Strategy for 8/5 Four of a Kind Bonus Poker

1 All pat hands…stand

2. Four cards to a royal flush…draw one card *(break anything else including a flush or straight)*

3. Four cards to a straight flush…draw one card *(break anything else)*

4. Three of a kind…draw two cards *(break anything except hands above)*

5. Four cards to a straight flush—inside draw…draw one card *(break anything except hands above)*

6. Two pairs…draw one card *(break anything except hands above)*

7. Pair of jacks or better…draw three cards *(break anything except hands above)*

8. Three cards to the royal flush…draw two cards *(break anything except hands above)*

9. Four cards to a flush…draw one card *(break anything except hands above)*

10. Four cards to a straight with two or three high cards—outside draw…draw one card *(break anything except hands above)*

11. Low pair…draw three cards *(break anything except hands above)*

12. Three cards to a straight flush—with one or more high cards—inside or outside draw…draw two cards *(break anything except hands above)*

13. Four cards to a straight with one or no high cards—outside draw…draw one card *(break anything except hands above)*

14. Three card straight flush—inside or outside draw…draw two cards *(break anything except hands above)*

15. Four cards to a straight with ace high—inside draw …draw one card *(break anything except hands above)*

16. Two cards to the royal flush…draw three cards *(break anything except hands above)*

17. Three cards to a straight flush—double inside draw …draw two cards *(break anything except hands above)*

18. One, two, or three high cards…draw four, three or two cards *(break anything except hands above)*

19. Four cards to a straight with three high cards—inside draw…draw one card *(break anything except hands above)*

20. All other hands…discard and draw five cards

All American (or 'Gator Poker) 8/8 Jacks or Better Draw Poker with 4,000 coins for Royal Flush 100.7% Payback

Royal Flush 800
Straight Flush 200
Four of a Kind 40
Full House 8
Flush 8
Straight 8
Three of a Kind 3
Two Pairs 1
Jacks or better 1

Strategy for All-American or 'Gator Poker

1. All pat hands…stand

2. Four cards to a royal flush…draw one card *(break anything else including a flush or straight)*

3. Four cards to a straight flush…draw one card *(break anything else including a flush or straight)*

4. Three of a kind...draw two cards

5. Three cards to a royal flush...draw two cards *(break anything except hands above)*

6. Two pairs...draw one card *(break anything except hands above)*

7. Four cards to a flush...draw one card *(break anything except hands above)*

8. Four cards to a straight—outside draw...draw one card *(break anything except hands above)*

9. Pair of jacks or better...draw three cards *(break anything except hands above)*

10. Three cards to a straight flush...draw two cards *(break anything except hands above)*

11. Four cards to a straight—inside draw...draw one card *(break anything except hands above)*

12. Three cards to a straight flush—double inside draw ...draw two cards *(break anything except hands above)*

13. Low pair...draw three cards *(break anything except hands above)*

14. Two cards to the royal flush with no 10...draw three cards *(break anything except hands above)*

15. Three cards to a straight (10, jack, queen)...draw two cards *(break anything except hands above)*

16. Three high cards with no ace...draw two cards *(break anything except hands above)*

17. Three cards to a flush with one or two high cards...draw two cards *(break anything except hands above)*

18. Three high cards including ace...draw two cards *(break anything except hands above)*

19. Three card straight (nine, ten, jack)...draw two cards *(break anything except hands above)*

20. Two cards to the royal flush with a 10...draw three cards *(break anything except hands above)*

21. One or two high cards...draw four or three cards *(break anything except hands above)*

22. Ace-10 of the same suit…draw three cards *(break anything except hands above)*

23. Three cards to a straight…draw two cards *(break anything except hands above)*

24. Three cards to a flush…draw two cards *(break anything except hands above)*

25. Two cards to a straight flush…draw three cards *(break anything except hands above)*

26. All other hands…discard and draw five cards

All American (or 'Gator Poker) Version II
8/8 Jacks or Better Draw Poker with 4,000 coins for Royal Flush 98.5% Payback

Royal Flush 800
Straight Flush 200
Four of a Kind 30
Full House 8
Flush 8
Straight 8
Three of a Kind 3
Two Pairs 1
Jacks or better 1

Strategy for Version II: All-American or 'Gator Poker

1. All pat hands…stand

2. Four cards to a royal flush…draw one card *(break anything else including a flush or straight)*

3. Four cards to a straight flush…draw one card *(break anything else including a flush or straight)*

4. Three of a kind…draw two cards

5. Three cards to a royal flush...draw two cards *(break anything except hands above)*

6. Two pairs...draw one card *(break anything except hands above)*

7. Four cards to a flush...draw one card *(break anything except hands above)*

8. Four cards to a straight—outside draw...draw one card *(break anything except hands above)*

9. Pair of jacks or better...draw three cards *(break anything except hands above)*

10. Three cards to a straight flush...draw two cards *(break anything except hands above)*

11. Four cards to a straight—inside draw...draw one card *(break anything except hands above)*

12. Three cards to a straight flush—double inside draw ...draw two cards *(break anything except hands above)*

13. Low pair...draw three cards *(break anything except hands above)*

14. Two cards to the royal flush with no 10...draw three cards *(break anything except hands above)*

15. Three cards to a straight (10, jack, queen)...draw two cards *(break anything except hands above)*

16. Three high cards with no ace...draw two cards *(break anything except hands above)*

17. Three cards to a flush with one or two high cards...draw two cards *(break anything except hands above)*

18. Three high cards including ace...draw two cards *(break anything except hands above)*

19. Three card straight (nine, ten, jack)...draw two cards *(break anything except hands above)*

20. Two cards to the royal flush with a 10...draw three cards *(break anything except hands above)*

21. One or two high cards...draw four or three cards *(break anything except hands above)*

22. Ace-10 of the same suit...draw three cards *(break anything except hands above)*

23. Three cards to a straight...draw two cards *(break anything except hands above)*

24. Three cards to a flush...draw two cards *(break anything except hands above)*

25. Two cards to a straight flush...draw three cards *(break anything except hands above)*

26. All other hands...discard and draw five cards

Group B: Play If You Must Jacks or Better Machines 95% to 97.9% Return

8/5 Jacks or Better with 4,000 coins for Royal Flush 97.3% Payback

Royal Flush 800
Straight Flush 50
Four of a Kind 25
Full House 8
Flush 5
Straight 4
Three of a Kind 3
Two Pairs 2
Jacks or Better 1

Strategy for 8/5 Jacks or Better

1. All pat hands...stand

2. Four cards to a royal flush...draw one card *(break anything else including a flush or a straight)*

3. Three of a kind...draw two cards

4. Four cards to a straight flush...draw one card *(break anything except hands above)*

5. Two pairs...draw one card

6. Four cards to a straight flush—inside draw...draw one card

7. Jacks or better...draw three cards

8. Three cards to the royal flush...draw two cards *(break anything except hands above)*

9. Four cards to a flush...draw one card *(break anything except hands above)*

10. Four cards to a straight with two or three high cards—outside draw...draw one card *(break anything except hands above)*

11. Low pair...draw three cards

12. Four cards to a straight with fewer than two high cards—outside draw...draw one card *(break anything except hands above)*

13. Three cards to a straight flush...draw two cards *(break anything except hands above)*

14. Four cards to a straight with ace high—inside draw ...draw one card *(break anything except hands above)*

15. Two cards to a royal...draw three cards *(break anything except hands above)*

16. One, two or three high cards...draw four, three or two cards *(break anything except hands above)*

17. Four cards to a straight with three high cards—inside draw...draw one card *(break anything except hands above)*

18. Three cards to a flush—inside draws...draw two cards *(break anything except hands above)*

19. All other hands...discard and draw five cards

6/5 Jacks or Better Draw Poker with 5,000 coins for Royal Flush 95.5% Payback

Royal Flush 1,000
Straight Flush 50
Four of a Kind 25
Full House 6
Flush 5
Straight 4
Three of a Kind 3
Two Pairs 2
Jacks or Better 1

Strategy for 6/5 Jacks or Better

1. All pat hands...stand

2. Four cards to a royal flush...draw one card (*break anything including a flush or straight*)

3. Three of a kind...draw two cards

4. Four cards to a straight flush...draw one card (*break anything except hands above*)

5. Two pairs...draw one card

6. Four cards to a straight flush—inside draw...draw one card (*break anything except hands above*)

7. Three cards to a royal flush...draw two cards (*break anything except hands above*)

8. Pair of jacks or better...draw three cards (*break anything except hands above*)

9. Four cards to a flush...draw one card (*break anything except hands above*)

10. Four cards to a straight with two or three high cards—outside draw...draw one card (*break anything except hands above*)

11. Low pair...draw three cards (*break anything except hands above*)

12. Four cards to a straight with fewer than two high cards—outside draw…draw one card

13. Three cards to a straight flush—inside or outside draw …draw two cards (*break anything except hands above*)

14. Four cards to a straight with an ace—inside draw…draw one card (*break anything except hands above*)

15. Two cards to a royal flush…draw three cards (*break anything except hands above*)

16. One, two, or three high cards…draw four, three or two cards (*break anything except hands above*)

17. Four cards to a straight with three high cards—inside draw…draw one card (*break anything except hands above*)

18. All other hands…discard and draw five cards

Megapoker Jacks or Better Linked Progressive with $20,000 starting Jackpot 97.6% to 98.26% Payback

Royal Flush in sequence . . Progressive Jackpot
Royal Flush 800
Straight Flush 50
Four of a Kind 25
Full House 8
Flush 5
Straight 4
Three of a Kind 3
Two Pairs 2
Jacks or Better 1

Strategy for Megapoker

1. All pat hands…stand

2. Three or four cards to a sequential royal flush…draw

two or one cards *(break anything else including a flush or straight)*

3. Four cards to a royal flush…draw one card *(break anything else including a flush or straight)*

4. Three of a kind…draw two cards

5. Four cards to a straight flush…draw one card *(break anything except hands above)*

6. Two pairs…draw one card

7. Four cards to a straight flush—inside draw…draw one card *(break anything except hands above)*

8. Jacks or better…draw three cards *(break anything except hands above)*

9. Three cards to a royal flush…draw two cards *(break anything except hands above)*

10. Four cards to a flush…draw one card *(break anything except hands above)*

11. Two cards to a sequential royal flush…draw three cards *(break anything except hands above)*

12. Four cards to a straight with two or three high cards—outside draw…draw one car *(break anything except hands above)*

13. Low pair…draw three cards *(break anything except hands above)*

14. Four cards to a straight—outside draw…draw one card *(break anything except hands above)*

15. Three cards to a straight flush—inside or outside draw…draw two cards *(break anything except hands above)*

16. Four cards to a straight with ace high—inside draw…draw one card *(break anything except hands above)*

17. Two cards to a royal flush…draw three cards *(break anything except hands above)*

18. One, two, or three high cards…draw four, three, or two cards *(break anything except hands above)*

19. Four cards to a straight with three high cards—inside draw…draw one card *(break anything except hands above)*

20. Three cards to a straight flush—inside draws…draw two cards *(break anything except hands above)*

21. All other hands…discard and draw five cards

Pokermania
Jacks or Better Draw Poker with Progressive Jackpot for Selected Suited Sequential and None-Selected Suited Sequential Royal Flush— Jackpot starts at $100,000 95.8% to 98.5% Payback

(Note: The machine designates which sequential royal flush it will pay the jackpot to. All other sequential royal flushes are paid a secondary jackpot. What are the odds of getting a preselected sequential? Hold your breath—it's 17,000,000 to one! Any other sequential is a mere 4,700,000 to one. By way of comparison, the New York State Lottery odds are 12,900,000 to one and its jackpot starts at $2,500,000 and sometimes goes higher than the $40,000,000 mark.)

Selected Sequential Royal Flush	Main Progressive Jackpot
Sequential Royal	Second Progressive Jackpot
Royal Flush	800
Straight Flush	50
Four of a Kind	25
Full House	6
Flush	5
Straight	4
Three of a Kind	3
Two Pairs	2
Jacks or Better	1

Strategy for Pokermania

1. All pat hands...stand

2. Four cards in sequence of selected suit...draw one card *(break anything else including a straight flush, flush or straight)*

3. Three cards in sequence of selected suit...draw two cards *(break anything else including a straight flush, flush or straight)*

4. Four cards in sequence of non-selected suit...draw one card *(break anything else including a straight flush, flush or straight)*

5. Four cards to a royal flush...draw one card *(break anything else including a flush or straight)*

6. Two cards in sequence of selected suit...draw three cards *(break anything else, including a straight, except hands above)*

7. Three of a kind...draw two cards

8. Four cards to a straight flush...draw one card *(break anything else except hands above)*

9. Three cards to a non-selected sequential royal flush...draw two cards *(break anything else except hands above)*

10. Two pairs...draw one card

11. Four cards to a straight flush—inside draw...draw one card *(break anything else except hands above)*

12. Jacks or better...draw three cards *(break anything else except hands above)*

13. Three cards to a royal flush...draw two cards *(break anything else except hands above)*

14. Four cards to a flush...draw one card *(break anything else except hands above)*

15. Four cards to a straight with two or three high cards—outside draw...draw one card *(break anything else except hands above)*

16. Low pair...draw three cards *(break anything else except hands above)*

17. Four cards to a straight with fewer than two high cards—outside draw...draw one card *(break anything else except hands above)*

18. Three cards to a straight flush...draw two cards (*break anything else except hands above*)

19. Two cards to a non-selected royal flush with no ace or ten...draw three cards (*break anything else except hands above*)

20. Four cards to a straight with ace high—inside draw...draw one card (*break anything else except hands above*)

21. Two cards to a royal flush...draw three cards (*break anything else except hands above*)

22. Four cards to a straight—inside draw...draw one card (*break anything else except hands above*)

23. Any card of selected sequential royal in the proper sequence...draw four cards (*break anything else except hands above*)

24. One, two or three high cards...draw four, three or two cards

25. All other hands...discard and draw five cards

Bonus Deuces Four of a Kind Jacks or Better Draw Poker with 4,000 coins for Royal Flush 96.8% Payback

Royal Flush 800
Straight Flush 50
Four Deuces 80
Four 3's, 4's, 5's 40
Four of a Kind 25
Full House 6
Flush 5
Straight 4
Three of a Kind 3
Two Pairs 2
Jacks or Better 1

Strategy for Bonus Deuces

1. All pat hands...stand

2. Four cards to a royal flush...draw one card *(break anything else including a flush or a straight)*

3. Three of a kind...draw two cards

4. Four cards to a straight flush—inside or outside draw ...draw one card *(break anything else except hands above)*

5. Two pairs...draw one card

6. Three cards to a royal flush...draw two cards *(break anything else except hands above)*

7. Jacks or better...draw three cards *(break anything else except hands above)*

8. Four cards to a flush...draw one card *(break anything else except hands above)*

9. Pair of deuces...draw three cards *(break anything else except hands above)*

10. Four cards to a straight with two or three high cards— outside draw...draw one card *(break anything else except hands above)*

11. Low pair...draw three cards *(break anything else except hands above)*

12. Four cards to a straight with fewer than two high cards— outside draw...draw one card *(break anything else except hands above)*

13. Three cards to a straight flush...draw two cards *(break anything else except hands above)*

14. Four cards to a straight with ace high—inside draw...draw one card *(break anything else except hands above)*

15. Two cards to a royal flush...draw three cards *(break anything else except hands above)*

16. Four cards to a straight with three high cards—inside draw...draw one card *(break anything else except hands above)*

17. One, two or three high cards...draw four, three or two cards *(break anything else except hands above)*

18. Three cards to a straight flush—inside draws…draw two cards *(break anything else except hands above)*

19. All other hands…discard and draw five cards

Group C
Don't Play These Machines
94.9% or Lower Returns

Louisiana Jacks Draw Poker with 2,500 coins for the Royal Flush 94% Payback

```
Royal Flush . . . . . . . . . . . . . . . . . . . . . . . . 500
Straight Flush . . . . . . . . . . . . . . . . . . . . . . 75
Four of a Kind  . . . . . . . . . . . . . . . . . . . . . 35
Full House  . . . . . . . . . . . . . . . . . . . . . . . . 9
Flush  . . . . . . . . . . . . . . . . . . . . . . . . . . . 6
Straight  . . . . . . . . . . . . . . . . . . . . . . . . . 4
Three of a Kind  . . . . . . . . . . . . . . . . . . . . 2
Two Pairs . . . . . . . . . . . . . . . . . . . . . . . . . 2
Jacks or Better  . . . . . . . . . . . . . . . . . . . . . 1
```

Louisiana Bonus Jacks or Better Draw Poker with 2,500 coins for the Royal Flush 92.6% Payback

```
Royal Flush . . . . . . . . . . . . . . . . . . . . . . . 500
Straight Flush . . . . . . . . . . . . . . . . . . . . . . 75
Four Aces . . . . . . . . . . . . . . . . . . . . . . . . . 80
Four K's, Q's, J's  . . . . . . . . . . . . . . . . . . . 40
Four 2's-10's. . . . . . . . . . . . . . . . . . . . . . . 25
```

Full House 8
Flush 6
Straight 4
Three of a Kind 2
Two Pairs 2
Jacks or Better 1

Player's Choice Jacks or Better Draw Poker with 2,500 coins for Royal Flush
94% Payback

Royal Flush 500
Straight Flush 100
Four of a Kind 25
Full House 10
Flush 8
Straight 6
Three of a Kind 3
Two Pairs 1
Jacks or Better 1

Player's Choice Jacks or Better Draw Poker with 2,500 coins for Royal Flush—Version II
94.6% Payback

Royal Flush 500
Straight Flush 100
Four of a Kind 35
Full House 10
Flush 7
Straight 6
Three of a Kind 3
Two Pairs 1

4

Victory at Joker Poker

Joker Poker or Joker Wild Poker is the most popular form of video-poker game currently extant and its popularity is still growing. That's because the player has so many more options and alternatives with the addition of the wild-card joker. Couple that with the fact that expert play on some machines can yield upwards of 102% and you can see why this game continues to gain in popularity.

That's the good news.

The bad news is that Joker Poker is a highly volatile game—with drastic and long losing streaks punctuated by sudden, explosive wins. Bradley Davis in his excellent source book, *Mastering Joker Wild Video Poker* (Applied Technology Press, 1990), gives the players attempting this version of video-poker short-term expectation figures—to enlighten them as to just what the average experience is on these volatile machines. Davis' figures are nothing if not startling.

According to Davis, the best short-run expectation is on the 20-8-7-6 Two-Pairs-or-Better

Joker-Poker machines with the Natural Royal Flush paying 5,000 coins. You will win 45% of the time and lose 55% of the time. These machines will pay back, in the long run, up to that 102% figure. The worst machines in terms of their short-term paybacks are the 6-4-3-3 Jacks-or-Better Joker-Poker machines with their 12% win and 88% loss rate and the 15-6-4-3 Two-Pairs-or-Better Joker-Poker machines with their 16% win and 84% loss rate. In the long run these machines are no bargains either with their respective 92% and 90.5% total paybacks.

It bears repeating...in fact, it bears becoming a litany of sorts for the video-poker player: only play the best versions of the Joker Poker machines. Even on these you will, more often than not, go home a loser but in the long run you have an excellent chance to come out ahead. When the explosive winning sessions occur (and believe me, they do), you want to be within shooting distance of those long-run wins. You can do this by keeping your losses to a minimum by playing the best strategies on the best machines. And like all video poker, the actual name of the machine is not as important as the payout scale. For convenience's sake I have listed part of the payout scale in the title of the machine—giving you the figures for the Four of a Kind, Full House, Flush and Straight.

The approaches to Joker Poker (and any wild-card game) are somewhat more complex because you must divide your strategies into two categories. Category "A" will be initial hands that do *not* contain a joker. Category "B" will be initial hands that do contain a joker. One hard and fast law holds for Joker Poker and that is—never discard a joker!

Group A:
Machines You Should Play
98% to 102% Paybacks

Kings or Better: 20-7-5-3
Joker Poker with 5,000 coins
for Natural Royal Flush
101.1% Payback

Natural Royal Flush 1,000*
Five of a Kind 200
Joker Royal Flush 100
Straight Flush 50
Four of a Kind 20
Full House 7
Flush 5
Straight 3
Three of a Kind 2
Two Pairs 1
Kings or Better 1

Kings or Better: 20-7-5-3 Joker Poker with 4,700 coins for Natural Royal Flush *101% Payback*

Natural Royal Flush 940*
Five of a Kind 200
Joker Royal Flush 100
Straight Flush 50
Four of a Kind 20
Full House 7
Flush 5
Straight 3
Three of a Kind 2
Two Pairs 1
Kings or Better 1

Kings or Better: 20-7-5-3 Joker Poker with 4,000 coins for Natural Royal Flush *100.6% Payback*

Natural Royal Flush 800*
Five of a Kind 200
Joker Royal Flush 100
Straight Flush 50
Four of a Kind 20
Full House 7
Flush 5
Straight 3
Three of a Kind 2
Two Pairs 1
Kings or Better 1

(*Progressives must be at the following minimum levels for 100%+ paybacks: Nickels—$144; Quarters—$715; Dollars—$2,850.)

Kings or Better: 17-7-5-3 Joker Poker with 5,000 coins for Natural Royal Flush 98.5% Payback

Natural Royal Flush 1,000*
Five of a Kind 200
Joker Royal Flush 100
Straight Flush 50
Four of a Kind 17
Full House 7
Flush 5
Straight 3
Three of a Kind 2
Two Pairs 1
Kings or Better 1

Kings or Better: 17-7-5-3 Joker Poker with 4,700 coins for Natural Royal Flush 98.4% Payback

Natural Royal Flush 940*
Five of a Kind 200
Joker Royal Flush 100
Straight Flush 50
Four of a Kind 17
Full House 7
Flush 5
Straight 3
Three of a Kind 2
Two Pairs 1
Kings or Better 1

Kings or Better: 17-7-5-3
Joker Poker with 4,000 coins
for Natural Royal Flush
98.5% Payback

Natural Royal Flush 800*
Five of a Kind 200
Joker Royal Flush 100
Straight Flush 50
Four of a Kind 17
Full House 7
Flush 5
Straight 3
Three of a Kind 2
Two Pairs 1
Kings or Better 1

(*Progressives must be at the following minimum levels for 100%+ paybacks: Nickels—$392; Quarters—$1960; Dollars—$7,825.)

Kings or Better: 15-8-5-3
Joker Poker with 5,000 coins
for Natural Royal Flush
98.4% Payback

Natural Royal Flush 1,000*
Five of a Kind 200
Joker Royal Flush 100
Straight Flush 50
Four of a Kind 15
Full House 8
Flush 5
Straight 3
Three of a Kind 2
Two Pairs 1
Kings or Better 1

Kings or Better: 15-8-5-3 Joker Poker with 4,700 coins for Natural Royal Flush 98.2% Payback

Natural Royal Flush 940*
Five of a Kind 200
Joker Royal Flush 100
Straight Flush 50
Four of a Kind 15
Full House 8
Flush 5
Straight 3
Three of a Kind 2
Two Pairs 1
Kings or Better 1

Kings or Better: 15-8-5-3 Joker Poker with 4,000 coins for Natural Royal Flush 97.9% Payback

Natural Royal Flush 800*
Five of a Kind 200
Joker Royal Flush 100
Straight Flush 50
Four of a Kind 15
Full House 8
Flush 5
Straight 3
Three of a Kind 2
Two Pairs 1
Kings or Better 1

(*Progressives must be at the following minimum levels for 100%+ paybacks: Nickels—$415; Quarters—$2071; Dollars—$8,285.)

Strategy for All Kings or Better Machines
Non-Joker Hands

1. All pat hands...stand

2. Four of a kind...draw one card

3. Four cards to a royal flush...draw one card *(break anything including a flush or straight)*

4. Three of a kind...draw two cards

5. Four cards to a straight flush—inside or outside draw ...draw one card *(break anything except hands above)*

6. Two pairs...draw one card

7. Three cards to a royal flush...draw two cards *(break anything except hands above)*

8. Two kings or two aces...draw three cards *(break anything except hands above)*

9. Four cards to a flush...draw one card *(break anything except hands above)*

10. Any pair...draw three cards *(break anything except hands above)*

11. Three cards to a straight flush—outside draw...draw two cards *(break anything except hands above)*

12. Four cards to a straight—outside draw...draw one card *(break anything except hands above)*

13. Three card straight flush—inside draws...draw two cards *(break anything except hands above)*

14. Two cards to a royal flush...draw three cards *(break anything except hands above)*

15. Ace and king...draw three cards *(break anything except hands above)*

16. Ace...draw four cards

17. All other hands...discard and draw five cards

Joker Hands

1. All pat hands...stand

2. Joker four of a kind...draw one card

3. Four cards to a joker royal flush...draw one card *(break anything including a joker straight or flush)*

4. Four cards to a joker straight flush—inside or outside draws...draw one card *(break anything except hands above)*

5. Joker three of a kind...draw two cards *(break anything except hands above)*

6. Four cards to a joker flush with an ace or king...draw one card *(break anything except hands above)*

7. Three cards to a joker royal flush...draw two cards *(break anything except hands above)*

8. Three cards to a joker straight flush...draw two cards *(break anything except hands above)*

9. High joker pair...draw three cards *(break anything except hands above)*

10. Four cards to a joker straight...draw one card *(break anything except hands above)*

11. Four cards to a joker flush...draw one card *(break anything except hands above)*

12. Joker plus 5 through 10...draw three cards

13. Joker plus garbage...draw four cards

Two Pairs or Better: 20-8-7-6 Joker Poker with 5,000 coins for Natural Royal Flush 102% Payback

Natural Royal Flush 1000*
Five of a Kind 100
Joker Royal Flush 50
Straight Flush 50
Four of a Kind 20
Full House 8
Flush 7
Straight 6
Three of a Kind 2
Two Pairs 1

Two Pairs or Better: 20-8-7-6 Joker Poker with 4,700 coins for Natural Royal Flush 101.9% Payback

Natural Royal Flush 940*
Five of a Kind 100
Joker Royal Flush 50
Straight Flush 50
Four of a Kind 20
Full House 8
Flush 7
Straight 6
Three of a Kind 2
Two Pairs 1

Two Pairs or Better: 20-8-7-6 Joker Poker with 4,000 coins for Natural Royal Flush 101.6% Payback

Natural Royal Flush 800*
Five of a Kind 100
Joker Royal Flush 50
Straight Flush 50
Four of a Kind 20
Full House 8
Flush 7
Straight 6
Three of a Kind 2
Two Pairs 1

(* Progressives must be at the following minimum levels for 101%+ payouts: Nickels—$130.00; Quarters—$647.00; Dollars—$2,590.00.)

Two Pairs or Better: 20-8-7-5 Joker Poker with 5,000 coins for Natural Royal Flush 99.1% Payback

Natural Royal Flush 1000*
Five of a Kind 100
Joker Royal Flush .50
Straight Flush 50
Four of a Kind 20
Full House 8
Flush 7
Straight 5
Three of a Kind 2
Two Pairs 1

Two Pairs or Better: 20-8-7-5 Joker Poker with 4,700 coins for Natural Royal Flush 98.9% Payback

Natural Royal Flush 940*
Five of a Kind 100
Joker Royal Flush 50
Straight Flush 50
Four of a Kind 20
Full House 8
Flush 7
Straight 5
Three of a Kind 2
Two Pairs 1

Two Pairs or Better: 20-8-7-5 Joker Poker with 4,000 coins for Natural Royal Flush 98.7% Payback

Natural Royal Flush 800*
Five of a Kind 100
Joker Royal Flush 50
Straight Flush 50
Four of a Kind 20
Full House 8
Flush 7
Straight 5
Three of a Kind 2
Two Pairs 1

(*Progressives must be at the following minimum levels for 100%+ payouts: Nickels—$375.00; Quarters—$1870.00; Dollars—$7,475.00.)

Strategy for Two Pairs or Better Joker Poker: All 20-8-7-6 and All 20-8-7-5 Machines

Non-Joker Hands

1. All pat hands...stand

2. Four cards to a royal flush...draw one card *(break anything else including a flush or straight)*

3. Four of a kind...draw one card

4. Four cards to a straight flush—inside or outside draw ...draw one card *(break anything except hands above)*

5. Three of a kind...draw two cards *(break anything except hands above)*

6. Two pairs...draw one card

7. Three cards to a royal flush...draw two cards *(break anything except hands above)*

8. Four cards to a flush...draw one card *(break anything except hands above)*

9. Four cards to a straight—outside draw...draw one card *(break anything except hands above)*

10. Three cards to a straight flush—inside or outside draw ...draw two cards *(break anything except hands above)*

11. Any pair...draw three cards *(break anything except hands above)*

12. Three cards to a straight flush—double-inside draw ...draw two cards *(break anything except hands above)*

13. Four cards to a straight—inside draw...draw one card *(break anything except hands above)*

14. Three cards to a flush...draw two cards *(break anything except hands above)*

15. Two cards to a royal flush...draw three cards *(break anything except hands above)*

16. Two cards to a straight flush—inside or outside draws...draw three cards *(break anything except hands above)*

17. Three cards to a straight—inside or outside draws...draw two cards

18. All other hands...discard and draw five cards

Joker Hands

1. All pat hands...stand

2. Joker four of a kind...draw one card

3. Four cards to a joker royal flush—inside or outside draw ...draw one card *(break anything else including joker straight)*

4. Four cards to a joker straight flush...draw one card *(break anything else except hands above)*

5. Joker three of a kind...draw three cards *(break anything else except hands above)*

6. Four cards to a joker flush...draw one card *(break anything else except hands above)*

7. Three cards to a joker straight flush—inside or outside draw...draw two cards *(break anything else except hands above)*

8. Four cards to a joker straight—inside or outside draw ...draw one card *(break anything else except hands above)*

9. Three cards to a joker straight...draw two cards *(break anything else except hands above)*

10. Joker plus 5 through 10...draw three cards

11. Joker plus garbage...draw four cards

Two Pairs or Better: 20-10-6-5 Joker Poker with 5,000 coins for Natural Royal Flush 99.8% Payback

Natural Royal Flush 1000*
Five of a Kind 100
Joker Royal Flush .50
Straight Flush 50
Four of a Kind 20
Full House 10
Flush 6
Straight 5
Three of a Kind 2
Two Pairs 1

Two Pairs or Better: 20-10-6-5 Joker Poker with 4,700 coins for Natural Royal Flush 99.7% Payback

Natural Royal Flush 940*
Five of a Kind 100
Joker Royal Flush 50
Straight Flush 50
Four of a Kind 20
Full House 10
Flush 6
Straight 5
Three of a Kind 2
Two Pairs 1

Two Pairs or Better: 20-10-6-5 Joker Poker with 4,000 coins for Natural Royal Flush 99.4% Payback

```
Natural Royal Flush . . . . . . . . . . . . . . . . . .800*
Five of a Kind . . . . . . . . . . . . . . . . . . . . . 100
Joker Royal Flush . . . . . . . . . . . . . . . . . . . .50
Straight Flush . . . . . . . . . . . . . . . . . . . . . .50
Four of a Kind . . . . . . . . . . . . . . . . . . . . . .20
Full House . . . . . . . . . . . . . . . . . . . . . . . .10
Flush . . . . . . . . . . . . . . . . . . . . . . . . . . . .6
Straight . . . . . . . . . . . . . . . . . . . . . . . . . .5
Three of a Kind . . . . . . . . . . . . . . . . . . . . .2
Two Pairs . . . . . . . . . . . . . . . . . . . . . . . . .1
```

(*Progressives must be at the following minimum levels for 100%+ payouts: Nickels—$280.00; Quarters—$1,400.00; Dollars—$5,410.00.)

Strategy for Two Pairs or Better: All 20-10-6-5 Joker Poker Machines

Non-Joker Hands

1. All pat hands…stand

2. Four of a kind…draw one card

3. Four cards to a royal flush…draw one card *(break anything else including a flush or a straight)*

4. Four cards to a straight flush…draw one card *(break anything else except hands above)*

5. Three of a kind…draw two cards *(break anything else except hands above)*

6. Two pairs…draw one card *(break anything else except hands above)*

7. Three cards to a royal flush…draw two cards *(break anything else except hands above)*

8. Four cards to a flush…draw one card *(break anything else except hands above)*

9. Four cards to a straight—outside draw…draw one card *(break anything else except hands above)*

10. Any pair…draw three cards *(break anything else except hands above)*

11. Three cards to a straight flush—inside or outside draws …draw two cards *(break anything else except hands above)*

12. Four cards to a straight—inside draw…draw one card *(break anything else except hands above)*

13. Two cards to a royal flush…draw three cards *(break anything else except hands above)*

14. Three cards to a flush…draw two cards *(break anything else except hands above)*

15. Two cards to a straight flush—inside or outside draws …draw three cards *(break anything else except hands above)*

16. Three cards to a straight—inside or outside draws…draw two cards *(break anything else except hands above)*

17. All other hands…discard and draw five cards

Joker Hands

1. All pat hands…stand

2. Joker four of a kind…draw one card

3. Four cards to a joker royal flush…draw one card *(break anything except hands above.)*

4. Four cards to a joker straight flush—inside or outside draw…draw one card *(break anything except hands above.)*

5. Joker three of a kind…draw two cards *(break anything except hands above.)*

6. Four cards to a joker straight—outside draw…draw one card *(break anything except hands above.)*

7. Three cards to a joker royal flush…draw two cards *(break anything except hands above.)*

8. Three cards to a joker straight flush…draw two cards *(break anything except hands above.)*

9. Four cards to a joker flush…draw one card *(break anything except hands above.)*

10. Three cards to a joker straight—inside or outside draws
    ...draw two cards *(break anything except hands above.)*

11. Joker high pair...draw three cards

12. Joker plus 5 through 10...draw three cards

13. Joker plus garbage...draw four cards

Two Pairs or Better: 16-8-5-4 Joker Poker with 5,000 Coins for Five of a Kind 98.9% Payback

```
Five of Kind  . . . . . . . . . . . . . . . . . . . . . .1,000*
Natural Royal Flush  . . . . . . . . . . . . . . . . . .100
Joker Royal Flush  . . . . . . . . . . . . . . . . . . .100
Straight Flush  . . . . . . . . . . . . . . . . . . . . .100
Four of a Kind  . . . . . . . . . . . . . . . . . . . . .16
Full House  . . . . . . . . . . . . . . . . . . . . . . . .8
Flush . . . . . . . . . . . . . . . . . . . . . . . . . . . .5
Straight  . . . . . . . . . . . . . . . . . . . . . . . . . 4
Three of a Kind  . . . . . . . . . . . . . . . . . . . . 2
Two Pair . . . . . . . . . . . . . . . . . . . . . . . . . 1
```

Two Pairs or Better: 16-8-5-4 Joker Poker with 4,700 Coins for Five of a Kind 98.3% Payback

Five of Kind 940*
Natural Royal Flush 100
Joker Royal Flush 100
Straight Flush 100
Four of a Kind 16
Full House 8
Flush 5
Straight 4
Three of a Kind 2
Two Pair 1

Two Pairs or Better: 16-8-5-4 Joker Poker with 4,000 Coins for Five of a Kind 97.1% Payback

Five of Kind 800*
Natural Royal Flush 100
Joker Royal Flush 100
Straight Flush 100
Four of a Kind 16
Full House 8
Flush 5
Straight 4
Three of a Kind 2
Two Pair 1

(*Progressives must be at the following minimum levels for a 100%+ payback: Nickels—$285; Quarters—$1,410; Dollars—$5,610.)

Strategy for Two Pairs or Better: All 16-8-5-4 Joker Poker Machines

Non-Joker Hands

1. All pat hands...stand

2. Four of a kind...draw one card

3. Four cards to any straight flush...draw one card (*break anything including a straight or a flush*)

4. Three of a kind...draw two cards

5. Two pairs...draw one card

6. Three cards to any straight flush—outside draw...draw two cards (*break anything except hands above*)

7. Four cards to a flush...draw one card (*break anything except hands above*)

8. Three cards to any straight flush—inside draw...draw two cards (*break anything except hands above*)

9. Four cards to a straight—outside draw...draw one card (*break anything except hands above*)

10. Any pair...draw three cards (*break anything except hands above*)

11. Three cards to any straight flush—double inside draws ...draw three cards (*break anything except hands above*)

12. Four cards to a straight—inside draw...draw one card (*break anything except hands above*)

13. Three cards to a flush...draw two cards (*break anything except hands above*)

14. Three cards to a straight—outside draw...draw two cards (*break anything except hands above*)

15. Two cards to any straight flush...draw three cards (*break anything except hands above*)

16. One card from 5-10...draw four cards

17. All other hands...discard and draw five cards

Joker Hands

1. All pat hands...stand

2. Four cards to any joker straight flush...draw one card *(break anything including a straight or a flush)*

3. Joker three of a kind...draw two cards *(break anything except hands above)*

4. Three cards to any joker straight flush...draw two cards *(break anything except hands above)*

5. Four cards to a joker flush...draw one card *(break anything except hands above)*

6. Four cards to a joker straight—inside or outside draw ...draw one card *(break anything except handsabove)*

7. Joker 5 through 10...draw three cards

8. Three cards to a joker straight...draw two cards. *(break anything except hands above)*

9. Four cards to a joker flush...draw one card *(break anything except hands above)*

10. Joker with jack or queen...draw three cards

11. Four cards to a joker flush...draw one card *(break anything except hands above)*

12. Joker plus garbage...draw four cards

Jacks or Better: 10-5-4-3 Joker Poker with 5,000 coins for Natural Royal Flush 98.6% Payback

Natural Royal Flush 1,000*
Five of a Kind 250
Joker Royal Flush 200
Straight Flush 50
Four of a Kind 10
Full House 5
Flush 4
Straight 3
Three of a Kind 2
Two Pair 1
Jacks or Better 1

Jacks or Better: 10-5-4-3 Joker Poker with 4,700 coins for Natural Royal Flush 98.4% Payback

Natural Royal Flush 940*
Five of a Kind 250
Joker Royal Flush 200
Straight Flush 50
Four of a Kind 10
Full House 5
Flush 4
Straight 3
Three of a Kind 2
Two Pair 1
Jacks or Better 1

Jacks or Better: 10-5-4-3 Joker Poker with 4,000 coins for Natural Royal Flush 98% Payback

Natural Royal Flush 800*
Five of a Kind 250
Joker Royal Flush 200
Straight Flush 50
Four of a Kind 10
Full House 5
Flush 4
Straight 3
Three of a Kind 2
Two Pair 1
Jacks or Better 1

(*Progressives must be at the following minimum levels for a 100%+ payback: Nickels—$380; Quarters—$1,900; Dollars—$7,575.)

Strategy for Jacks or Better: All 10-5-4-3 Machines

Non-Joker Hands

1. All pat hands…stand

2. Four cards to a royal flush…draw one card *(break anything including a flush or straight)*

3. Four of a kind…draw one card

4. Four cards to a straight flush—inside or outside draw…draw one card *(break anything except hands above)*

5. Three of a kind…draw two cards *(break anything except hands above)*

6. Three cards to a royal flush…draw two cards *(break anything except hands above)*

7. Two pair…draw three cards

8. Jacks or better…draw three cards *(break anything except hands above)*

9. Four cards to a flush…draw one card *(break anything except hands above)*

10. Four cards to a straight with two or three high cards—outside draw…draw one card *(break anything except hands above)*

11. Three cards to a straight flush…draw two cards *(break anything except hands above)*

12. Two cards to a royal flush…draw three cards *(break anything except hands above)*

13. Low pair…draw three cards *(break anything except hands above)*

14. Four cards to a straight with one or no high cards—outside draw…draw one card *(break anything except hands above)*

15. One jack or better…draw four cards

16. All other hands…discard and draw five cards

Joker Hands

1. All pat hands…stand

2. Joker four of a kind…draw one card

3. Four cards to a joker royal flush…draw one card *(break anything including flush or straight)*

4. Four cards to a joker straight flush…draw one card *(break anything including a straight or flush)*

5. Joker three of a kind…draw two cards *(break anything except hands above)*

6. Three cards to a joker royal flush…draw two cards *(break anything except hands above)*

7. Three cards to a joker straight flush…draw two cards *(break anything except hands above)*

8. Four cards to a joker straight—inside or outside draw …draw one card *(break anything except hands above)*

9. Four cards to a joker flush...draw one card *(break anything except hands above)*

10. Joker with a jack or better...draw three cards *(break anything except hands above)*

11. Joker with a 5 through 10...draw three cards

12. Joker with garbage...draw four cards

Group B: Play If You Must Joker Poker Machines 95% to 97.9% Return

Two Pairs or Better: 20-8-6-5 Joker Poker with 5,000 coins for Natural Royal Flush 96.8% Payback

Natural Royal Flush 1000*
Five of a Kind 100
Joker Royal Flush 50
Straight Flush 50
Four of a Kind 20
Full House 8
Flush 6
Straight 5
Three of a Kind 2
Two Pairs 1

Two Pairs or Better: 20-8-6-5 Joker Poker with 4,700 coins for Natural Royal Flush 96.7% Payback

Natural Royal Flush 940*
Five of a Kind 100
Joker Royal Flush 50
Straight Flush 50
Four of a Kind 20
Full House 8
Flush 6
Straight 5
Three of a Kind 2
Two Pairs 1

Two Pairs or Better: 20-8-6-5 Joker Poker with 4,000 coins for Natural Royal Flush 96.4% Payback

Natural Royal Flush 800*
Five of a Kind 100
Joker Royal Flush 50
Straight Flush 50
Four of a Kind 20
Full House 8
Flush 6
Straight 5
Three of a Kind 2
Two Pairs 1

(*Progressives must be at the following minimum levels for a 100%+ payback: Nickels—$594; Quarters—$2,970; Dollars—$11,880.)

Strategy for Two Pairs or Better
All 20-8-6-5 Machines

Non-Joker Hands

1. All pat hands...stand

2. Four cards to a royal flush...draw one card (*break anything including a flush or a straight*)

3. Four of a kind...draw one card

4. Four cards to a straight flush...draw one card (*break anything except hands above*)

5. Three of a kind...draw two cards (*break anything except hands above*)

6. Two pair...draw one card

7. Three cards to a royal flush...draw two cards (*break anything except hands above*)

8. Four cards to a flush...draw one card (*break anything except hands above*)

9. Four cards to a straight—outside draw...draw one card (*break anything except hands above*)

10. Three cards to a straight flush—outside draw...draw two cards (*break anything except hands above*)

11. Any pair...draw three cards (*break anything except hands above*)

12. Three cards to a straight flush...draw two cards (*break anything except hands above*)

13. Four cards to a straight—inside draw...draw one card (*break anything except hands above*)

14. Two cards to a royal flush...draw three cards (*break anything except hands above*)

15. Three cards to a flush...draw two cards (*break anything except hands above*)

16. Two cards to a straight flush...draw three cards (*break anything except hands above*)

17. Three cards to a straight—inside or outside draw…draw two cards

18. All other hands…discard and draw five cards

Joker Hands

1. All pat hands…stand

2. Joker four of a kind…draw one card

3. Four cards to a joker royal flush with queen high…draw one card *(break anything including a flush or a straight)*

4. Four cards to a joker straight flush—outside draw…draw one card *(break anything including a flush or a straight)*

5. Four cards to a joker royal flush with king high…draw one card *(break anything including a straight)*

6. Four cards to a joker straight flush—inside draw…draw one card *(break anything including a straight)*

7. Four cards to a joker royal flush with ace high…draw one card *(break anything except hands above)*

8. Four cards to a joker straight flush—double inside draw…draw one card *(break anything except hands above)*

9. Joker three of a kind…draw two cards *(break anything except hands above)*

10. Four cards to a joker straight—outside draw…draw one card *(break anything except hands above)*

11. Three cards to a joker royal flush…draw two cards *(break anything except hands above)*

12. Three cards to a joker straight flush…draw two cards *(break anything except hands above)*

13. Four cards to a joker flush…draw one card *(break anything except hands above)*

14. Four cards to a joker straight—inside draw…draw one card *(break anything except hands above)*

15. Three cards to a joker straight…draw two cards *(break anything except hands above)*

16. Three cards to a joker flush…draw two cards *(break anything except hands above)*

17. Joker plus 5 through 10…draw three cards *(break anything except hands above)*

18. Joker plus jack or queen…draw three cards

19. Joker plus garbage…draw four cards

Two Pairs or Better: 25-8-5-4 Joker Poker with 5,000 coins for Natural Royal Flush 96% Payback

Natural Royal Flush 1000*
Five of a Kind 100
Joker Royal Flush 50
Straight Flush 50
Four of a Kind 25
Full House 8
Flush 5
Straight 4
Three of a Kind 2
Two Pairs 1

Two Pairs or Better: 25-8-5-4 Joker Poker with 4,700 coins for Natural Royal Flush 95.9% Payback

Natural Royal Flush 940*
Five of a Kind 100
Joker Royal Flush 50
Straight Flush 50
Four of a Kind 25
Full House 8
Flush 5
Straight 4
Three of a Kind 2
Two Pairs 1

Two Pairs or Better: 25-8-5-4 Joker Poker with 4,000 coins for Natural Royal Flush 95.6% Payback

Natural Royal Flush 1000*
Five of a Kind 100
Joker Royal Flush 50
Straight Flush 50
Four of a Kind 25
Full House 8
Flush 5
Straight 4
Three of a Kind 2
Two Pairs 1

(*Progressives must be at the following minimum levels for a 100%+ payback: Nickels—$678; Quarters—$3,390; Dollars—$15,540.)

Strategy for Two Pairs or Better
All 25-8-5-4 Machines

Non-Joker Hands

1. All pat hands...stand

2. Four cards to a royal flush...draw one card *(break anything including a straight or flush)*

3. Four of a kind...draw one card

4. Four cards to a straight flush—outside draw...draw one card *(break anything including a straight)*

5. Three of a kind...draw two cards *(break anything except hands above)*

6. Four cards to a straight flush—inside draw...draw one card *(break anything except hands above)*

7. Two pairs...draw one card *(break anything except hands above)*

8. Three cards to a royal flush...draw two cards *(break anything except hands above)*

9. Four cards to a flush...draw one card *(break anything except hands above)*

10. Three cards to a straight flush—outside draw...draw two cards *(break anything except hands above)*

11. Any pair...draw three cards *(break anything except hands above)*

12. Four cards to a straight—outside draw...draw one card

13. Three cards to a straight flush—inside draws...draw two cards *(break anything except hands above)*

14. Four cards to a straight—inside draw...draw one card *(break anything except hands above)*

15. Two cards to a royal flush...draw three cards *(break anything except hands above)*

16. Three cards to a flush...draw two cards *(break anything except hands above)*

17. Two cards to a straight flush...draw three cards *(break anything except hands above)*

18. Three cards to a straight—outside draw...draw two cards *(break anything except hands above)*

19. One ten...draw four cards

20. All other hands...discard and draw five cards

Joker Hands

1. All pat hands...stand

2. Joker four of a kind...draw one card

3. Four cards to a joker royal flush (queen high) or straight flush—outside draw...draw one card *(break anything including a flush and straight)*

4. Four cards to a joker royal flush (king high) or straight flush—inside draw...draw one card *(break anything including a straight)*

5. Joker three of a kind...draw two cards *(break anything except hands above)*

6. Four cards to a joker royal flush...draw one card *(break anything except hands above)*

7. Four cards to a joker straight flush...draw one card *(break anything except hands above)*

8. Three cards to a joker royal flush (jack high)...draw two cards *(break anything except hands above)*

9. Three cards to a joker straight flush—outside draw...draw two cards *(break anything except hands above)*

10. Four cards to a joker straight—outside draw...draw one card *(break anything except hands above)*

11. Three cards to a joker royal flush (queen high)...draw two cards *(break anything except hands above)*

12. Three cards to a joker straight flush—inside draw...draw two cards *(break anything except hands above)*

13. Four cards to a joker flush...draw one card *(break anything except hands above)*

14. Three cards to a joker royal flush...draw two cards *(break anything except hands above)*

15. Three cards to a joker straight flush...draw two cards *(break anything except hands above)*

16. Four cards to a joker straight—inside draw...draw one card *(break anything except hands above)*

17. Joker plus 5 through 10...draw three cards *(break anything except hands above)*

18. Joker plus jack or queen high...draw three cards *(break anything except hands above)*

19. Three cards to a joker straight—outside draw...draw two cards *(break anything except hands above)*

20. Joker plus garbage...draw four cards

Two Pairs or Better: 25-5-4-3 Joker Poker with 4,000 coins for Natural and Joker-Royal Flushes 97.3% Payback

Natural Royal Flush 800
Joker Royal Flush 800
Five of a Kind 160
Straight Flush 80
Four of a Kind 25
Full House 5
Flush 4
Straight 3
Three of a Kind 2
Two Pairs 1

Strategy for Two Pairs or Better 25-5-4-3 Machines

Non-Joker Hands

1. All pat hands...stand

2. Four cards to a royal flush...draw one card (*break anything including a flush or straight*

3. Four of a kind...draw one card

4. Four cards to a straight flush—inside or outside draw ...draw one card (*break anything including a straight or a flush*)

5. Three of a kind...draw two cards (*break anything except hands above*)

6. Three cards to a royal flush...draw two cards (*break anything except hands above*)

7. Two pairs...draw one card (*break anything except hands above*)

8. Three cards to a straight flush...draw two cards (*break anything except hands above*)

9. Four cards to a flush...draw one card (*break anything except hands above*)

10. Any pair...draw three cards (*break anything except hands above*)

11. Three cards to a straight flush—inside draw...draw two cards (*break anything except hands above*)

12. Four cards to a straight...draw one card (*break anything except hands above*)

13. Three cards to a straight flush—double inside draw...draw two cards (*break anything except hands above*)

14. Two cards to a royal flush...draw three cards (*break anything except hands above*)

15. Four cards to a straight—inside draw...draw one card (*break anything except hands above*)

16. Two cards to a straight flush...draw three cards (*break anything except hands above*)

17. Three cards to a flush…draw two cards

18. All other hands…discard and draw five cards

Joker Hands

1. All pat hands…stand

2. Four cards to a joker royal flush…draw one card *(break anything including a straight or a flush)*

3. Joker four of a kind…draw one card

4. Four cards to a joker straight flush inside or outside draw…draw one card *(break anything including a straight or a flush)*

5. Joker three of a kind…draw two cards *(break anything except hands above)*

6. Three cards to a joker royal flush…draw two cards *(break anything, including a straight, except hands above)*

7. Three cards to a joker straight flush…draw two cards *(break anything except hands above)*

8. Four cards to a joker straight…draw one card *(break anything except hands above)*

9. Joker plus jack or better…draw three cards *(break anything except hands above)*

10. Joker plus 5 through 9…draw three cards *(break anything except hands above)*

11. Joker plus garbage…draw four cards

Kings or Better: 15-7-5-3 Joker Poker with 5,000 coins for Natural Royal Flush 96.8% Payback

Natural Royal Flush 1000*
Five of a Kind 200
Joker Royal Flush 100
Straight Flush 50
Four of a Kind 15
Full House 7
Flush 5
Straight 3
Three of a Kind 2
Two Pairs 1
Kings or Better 1

Kings or Better: 15-7-5-3 Joker Poker with 4,700 coins for Natural Royal Flush 96.7% Payback

Natural Royal Flush 940*
Five of a Kind 200
Joker Royal Flush 100
Straight Flush 50
Four of a Kind 15
Full House 7
Flush 5
Straight 3
Three of a Kind 2
Two Pairs 1
Kings or Better 1

Kings or Better: 15-7-5-3
Joker Poker with 4,000 coins
for Natural Royal Flush
96.3% Payback

Natural Royal Flush 800*
Five of a Kind 200
Joker Royal Flush 100
Straight Flush. 50
Four of a Kind 15
Full House 7
Flush 5
Straight 3
Three of a Kind 2
Two Pairs 1
Kings or Better 1

(*Progressives must be at the following minimum levels for a 100%+ payback: Nickels—$555; Quarters—$2,770; Dollars—$11,100.)

Kings or Better: 20-5-4-3
Joker Poker with 5,000 coins
for Natural Royal Flush
95.9% Payback

Natural Royal Flush 1000*
Five of a Kind 200
Joker Royal Flush 100
Straight Flush 40
Four of a Kind 20
Full House 5
Flush 4
Straight 3
Three of a Kind 2
Two Pairs 1
Kings or Better 1

Kings or Better: 20-5-4-3
Joker Poker with 4,700 coins
for Natural Royal Flush
95.7% Payback

Natural Royal Flush 940*
Five of a Kind 200
Joker Royal Flush 100
Straight Flush 40
Four of a Kind 20
Full House 5
Flush 4
Straight 3
Three of a Kind 2
Two Pairs 1
Kings or Better 1

Kings or Better: 20-5-4-3
Joker Poker with 4,000 coins
for Natural Royal Flush
95.4% Payback

Natural Royal Flush 800*
Five of a Kind 200
Joker Royal Flush 100
Straight Flush 40
Four of a Kind 20
Full House 5
Flush 4
Straight 3
Three of a Kind 2
Two Pairs 1
Kings or Better 1

(*Progressives must be at the following minimum levels for a 100%+ payback: Nickels—$678; Quarters—$3,390; Dollars—$13,550.)

Strategy for All Kings or Better Machines Non-Joker Hands

1. All pat hands…stand

2. Four of a Kind…draw one card

3. Four cards to a royal flush…draw one card *(break anything including a flush or straight)*

4. Three of a kind…draw two cards

5. Four cards to a straight flush—inside or outside draw …draw one card *(break anything except hands above)*

6. Two pairs…draw one card

7. Three cards to a royal flush…draw two cards *(break anything except hands above)*

8. Two kings or two aces…draw three cards *(break anything except hands above)*

9. Four cards to a flush…draw one card *(break anything except hands above)*

10. Any pair…draw three cards *(break anything except hands above)*

11. Three cards to a straight flush—outside draw…draw two cards *(break anything except hands above)*

12. Four cards to a straight—outside draw…draw one card *(break anything except hands above)*

13. Three card straight flush—inside draws…draw two cards *(break anything except hands above)*

14. Two cards to a royal flush…draw three cards *(break anything except hands above)*

15. Ace and king…draw three cards *(break anything except hands above)*

16. Ace…draw four cards

17. All other hands…discard and draw five cards

Joker Hands

1. All pat hands…stand

2. Joker four of a kind…draw one card

3. Four cards to a joker royal flush…draw one card *(break anything including a joker straight or flush)*

4. Four cards to a joker straight flush—inside or outside draws…draw one card *(break anything except hands above)*

5. Joker three of a kind…draw two cards *(break anything except hands above)*

6. Four cards to a joker flush with an ace or king…draw one card *(break anything except hands above)*

7. Three cards to a joker royal flush…draw two cards *(break anything except hands above)*

8. Three cards to a joker straight flush…draw two cards *(break anything except hands above)*

9. High joker pair…draw three cards *(break anything except hands above)*

10. Four cards to a joker straight…draw one card *(break anything except hands above)*

11. Four cards to a joker flush…draw one card *(break anything except hands above)*

12. Joker plus 5 through 10…draw three cards

13. Joker plus garbage…draw four cards

Group C:
Don't Play These Joker Poker Machines returning 94.9% or Less

Two Pairs or Better: 20-8-6-4 Joker Poker with 5,000 coins for Natural Royal Flush 94% Payback

Natural Royal Flush 1000
Five of a Kind 100
Joker Royal Flush 50
Straight Flush 50
Four of a Kind 20
Full House 8
Flush 6
Straight 4
Three of a Kind 2
Two Pairs 1

Two Pairs or Better: 20-8-6-4 Joker Poker with 4,700 coins for Natural Royal Flush 93.9% Payback

Natural Royal Flush 940
Five of a Kind 100
Joker Royal Flush 50
Straight Flush 50
Four of a Kind 20
Full House 8
Flush 6
Straight 4
Three of a Kind 2
Two Pairs 1

Two Pairs or Better: 20-8-6-4 Joker Poker with 4,000 coins for Natural Royal Flush 93.6% Payback

Natural Royal Flush 800
Five of a Kind 100
Joker Royal Flush 50
Straight Flush 50
Four of a Kind 20
Full House 8
Flush 6
Straight 4
Three of a Kind 2
Two Pairs 1

Two Pairs or Better: 15-6-5-4 Joker Poker with 4,700* coins for Five of a Kind 94.5% Payback

Five of a Kind 940
Royal Flush 100
Joker Royal Flush 100
Straight Flush 100
Four of a Kind 15
Full House 6
Flush 5
Straight 4
Three of a Kind 2
Two Pairs 1

*If you can find a 5,000 coin payoff this machine will return approximately 95%—still not a good bet.

Two Pairs or Better: 15-6-5-4 Joker Poker with 4,000 coins for Five of a Kind 93.3% Payback

Five of a Kind 800
Royal Flush 100
Joker Royal Flush 100
Straight Flush 100
Four of a Kind 15
Full House 6
Flush 5
Straight 4
Three of a Kind 2
Two Pairs 1

Two Pairs or Better: 20-8-5-4 Joker Poker with 5,000 coins for Natural Royal Flush 91.9% Payback

Natural Royal Flush 1000
Five of a Kind 100
Joker Royal Flush 50
Straight Flush 50
Four of a Kind 20
Full House 8
Flush 5
Straight 4
Three of a Kind 2
Two Pairs 1

Two Pairs or Better: 20-8-5-4 Joker Poker with 4,700 coins for Natural Royal Flush 91.8% Payback

Natural Royal Flush 940
Five of a Kind 100
Joker Royal Flush 50
Straight Flush 50
Four of a Kind 20
Full House 8
Flush 5
Straight 4
Three of a Kind 2
Two Pairs 1

Two Pairs or Better: 20-8-5-4 Joker Poker with 4,000 coins for Natural Royal Flush 91.5% Payback

Natural Royal Flush 800
Five of a Kind 100
Joker Royal Flush 50
Straight Flush 50
Four of a Kind 20
Full House 8
Flush 5
Straight 4
Three of a Kind 2
Two Pairs 1

Two Pairs or Better: 20-10-4-3 Joker Poker with 5,000 coins for Natural Royal Flush 90.4% Payback

Natural Royal Flush 1000
Five of a Kind 100
Joker Royal Flush 50
Straight Flush 50
Four of a Kind 20
Full House 10
Flush 4
Straight 3
Three of a Kind 2
Two Pairs 1

Two Pairs or Better: 20-10-4-3 Joker Poker with 4,700 coins for Natural Royal Flush 90.3% Payback

Natural Royal Flush 940
Five of a Kind 100
Joker Royal Flush 50
Straight Flush 50
Four of a Kind 20
Full House 10
Flush 4
Straight 3
Three of a Kind 2
Two Pairs 1

Two Pairs or Better: 20-10-4-3 Joker Poker with 4,000 coins for Natural Royal Flush 89.9% Payback

Natural Royal Flush 800
Five of a Kind 100
Joker Royal Flush 50
Straight Flush 50
Four of a Kind 20
Full House 10
Flush 4
Straight 3
Three of a Kind 2
Two Pairs 1

Two Pairs or Better: 15-6-4-3 Joker Poker with 5,000 coins for Five of a Kind 90.5% Payback

Five of a Kind 1,000
Natural Royal Flush 100
Joker Royal Flush 100
Straight Flush 100
Four of a Kind 15
Full House 6
Flush 4
Straight 3
Three of a Kind 2
Two Pairs 1

Two Pairs or Better: 15-6-4-3 Joker Poker with 4,700 coins for Five of a Kind 90% Payback

Five of a Kind 940
Natural Royal Flush 100
Joker Royal Flush 100
Straight Flush 100
Four of a Kind 15
Full House 6
Flush 4
Straight 3
Three of a Kind 2
Two Pairs 1

Two Pairs or Better: 15-6-4-3
Joker Poker with 4,000 coins
for Five of a Kind
88.7% Payback

Five of a Kind 800
Natural Royal Flush 100
Joker Royal Flush 100
Straight Flush 100
Four of a Kind 15
Full House 6
Flush 4
Straight 3
Three of a Kind 2
Two Pairs 1

Jacks or Better: 6-4-3-3
Joker Poker with 5,000 coins
for Natural Royal Flush
92.1% Payback

Natural Royal Flush 1,000
Five of a Kind 250
Joker Royal Flush 200
Straight Flush 50
Four of a Kind 6
Full House 4
Flush 3
Straight 3
Three of a Kind 2
Two Pair 1
Jacks or Better 1

Jacks or Better: 6-4-3-3
Joker Poker with 4,700 coins
for Natural Royal Flush
92% Payback

Natural Royal Flush 940
Five of a Kind 250
Joker Royal Flush 200
Straight Flush 50
Four of a Kind 6
Full House 4
Flush 3
Straight 3
Three of a Kind 2
Two Pair 1
Jacks or Better 1

Jacks or Better: 6-4-3-3
Joker Poker with 4,000 coins
for Natural Royal Flush
91.6% Payback

Natural Royal Flush 800
Five of a Kind 250
Joker Royal Flush 200
Straight Flush 50
Four of a Kind 6
Full House 4
Flush 3
Straight 3
Three of a Kind 2
Two Pair 1
Jacks or Better 1

Jacks or Better: 10-6-4-3
Joker Poker with 1,250 coins
for Natural Royal Flush on five-coin
play and 2,000 on eight-coin play
94.7% Payback

Natural Royal Flush 250
Five of a Kind 120
Joker Royal Flush 80
Straight Flush 30
Four of a Kind 10
Full House 6
Flush 4
Straight 3
Three of a Kind 2
Two Pair 1
Jacks or Better 1

Aces or Better: 20-6-5-4
Joker Poker with 1,250 coins
for Natural Royal Flush on five-coin
play and 2,000 on eight-coin play
94.7% Payback

Natural Royal Flush 250
Five of a Kind 185
Joker Royal Flush 100
Straight Flush 50
Four of a Kind 20
Full House 6
Flush 5
Straight 4
Three of a Kind 2
Two Pair 1
Aces or Better 1

Aces or Better: 20-6-5-3 Joker Poker with 5,000 coins for Natural Royal Flush 94.3% Payback

Natural Royal Flush 1000
Five of a Kind 200
Joker Royal Flush 100
Straight Flush 50
Four of a Kind 20
Full House 6
Flush 5
Straight 3
Three of a Kind 2
Two Pair 1
Aces or Better 1

Aces or Better: 20-6-5-3 Joker Poker with 4,700 coins for Natural Royal Flush 94.1% Payback

Natural Royal Flush 940
Five of a Kind 200
Joker Royal Flush 100
Straight Flush 50
Four of a Kind 20
Full House 6
Flush 5
Straight 3
Three of a Kind 2
Two Pair 1
Aces or Better 1

Aces or Better: 20-6-5-3
Joker Poker with 4,000 coins
for Natural Royal Flush
93.8% Payback

Natural Royal Flush 800
Five of a Kind 200
Joker Royal Flush 100
Straight Flush 50
Four of a Kind 20
Full House 6
Flush 5
Straight 3
Three of a Kind 2
Two Pair 1
Aces or Better 1

5

Victory at *Deuces Wild* Video Poker

In the local neighborhood games where many a poker player cuts his or her gambling teeth, wild-card games are the norm. For some reason inexperienced players love them—perhaps because of the ease with which seemingly good hands can be made when, for example, all the deuces are wild. The fact that other players can also just as easily make good hands seems to elude them. The same basic appeal of the wild-card games seems to have informed the public's perception of video poker. It's easier to make good hands with the four deuces being wild. Of course, to win even a minimal amount at deuces-wild video poker you have to have even better hands than you do in Jacks-or-Better or Joker Poker. That's because those four deuces come out often.

Still, for expert players, deuces-wild video poker offers games with generous payouts climbing up to the 102 percentage mark. Once again the game is highly volatile and you can expect more losing sessions than winning ones—but those winning ones will more than likely be explosive.

Machines You Should Play Machines with Paybacks of 98% to 102%

Deuces Wild Three of a Kind or Better: 9-5-3-2 Machines with 4,000 coins for Royal Flush 100.6% Payback

Royal Flush 800
Four Deuces 200
Deuces Royal Flush 25
Five of a Kind 15
Straight Flush 9
Four of a Kind 5
Full House 3
Flush 2
Straight 2
Three of a Kind 1

Strategy for Deuces Wild 9-5-3-2 Machines

Non-Deuce Hands

1. All pat hands…stand

2. Four cards to a royal flush…draw one card *(break any-thing including a straight, flush, or a straight flush)*

3. Four of a kind…draw one card

4. Three of a kind…draw two cards

5. Four cards to a straight flush—inside or outside draw …draw one card *(break anything except hands above)*

6. Three cards to a royal flush…draw two cards *(break any-thing except hands above)*

7. One or two pairs…draw three or one card *(break anything except hands above)*

8. Four cards to a straight—outside draw…draw one card *(break anything except hands above)*

9. Four cards to a flush…draw one card *(break anything except hands above)*

10. Three cards to a straight flush—inside or outside draw …draw two cards *(break anything except hands above)*

11. Two cards to a royal flush with a jack or queen high …draw three cards *(break anything except hands above)*

12. Four cards to an straight—inside draw…draw one card *(break anything except hands above)*

13. All other hands…discard and draw five cards

Deuce Hands

1. All pat hands…stand

2. Three deuces and two garbage cards…draw two cards

3. Four of a kind with one or two deuces…draw one card

4. Four cards to a royal with one or two deuces…draw one card *(break anything except hands above)*

5. Two deuces and three garbage cards…draw three cards *(break anything except hands above)*

6. Four cards to a deuce straight flush…draw one card *(break anything except hands above)*

7. Three of a kind with one deuce…draw two cards

8. Four cards to a one-deuce straight flush—inside or outside draw…draw one card *(break anything except hands above)*

9. Three cards to a one-deuce royal flush…draw two cards *(break anything except hands above)*

10. One deuce plus garbage…draw four cards

Deuces Wild Three of a Kind or Better: 10-10-4-4 Machines with 4,000 coins for Royal Flush 101% Payback

Royal Flush 800
Four Deuces 400
Deuces Royal Flush 20
Five of a Kind 10
Straight Flush 10
Four of a Kind 4
Full House 4
Flush 3
Straight 2
Three of a Kind 1

Strategy for Deuces Wild 10-10-4-4 Machines

Non-Deuce Hands

1. All pat hands…stand

2. Four cards to a royal flush…draw one card *(break anything including a straight, flush, or a straight flush)*

3. Four of a kind…draw one card

4. Four cards to a straight flush—inside or outside draw …draw one card *(break anything except hands above)*

5. Three of a kind…draw two cards

6. Three cards to a royal flush…draw two cards *(break anything except hands above)*

7. Four cards to a flush…draw one card *(break anything except hands above)*

8. One or two pairs…draw three or one card *(break anything except hands above)*

9. Three cards to a straight flush—inside or outside draw …draw two cards *(break anything except hands above)*

10. Four cards to a straight...draw one card *(break anything except hands above)*

11. Two cards to a royal flush with a jack or queen high ...draw three cards *(break anything except hands above)*

12. All other hands...discard and draw five cards

Deuce Hands

1. All pat hands...stand

2. Three deuces and two garbage cards...draw two cards

3. Four of a kind with one or two deuces...draw one card

4. Four cards to a royal with one or two deuces...draw one card *(break anything except hands above)*

5. Two deuces and three garbage cards...draw three cards *(break anything except hands above)*

6. Four cards to a one-deuce straight flush...draw one card *(break anything except hands above)*

7. Three of a kind with one deuce...draw two cards

8. Three cards to a one-deuce royal flush...draw two cards *(break anything except hands above)*

9. One deuce plus garbage...draw four cards

Deuces Wild Three of a Kind or Better: 10-8-4-3 Machines with 4,000 coins for Royal Flush 100% Payback

Royal Flush 800
Four Deuces 600
Deuces Royal Flush 20
Five of a Kind 10
Straight Flush 8
Four of a Kind 4
Full House 3
Flush 2
Straight 2
Three of a Kind 1

Strategy for Deuces Wild 10-8-4-3 Machines

Non-Deuce Hands

1. All pat hands…stand

2. Four cards to a royal flush…draw one card (break anything including a straight, flush, or a straight flush)

3. Four of a kind…draw one card

4. Three of a kind…draw two cards

5. Four cards to a straight flush—inside or outside draw …draw one card (break anything except hands above)

6. Three cards to a royal flush…draw two cards (break anything except hands above)

7. Three cards to a straight flush—inside or outside draw …draw two cards (break anything except hands above)

8. One or two pairs…draw three or one card (break anything except hands above)

9. Four cards to a flush…draw one card (break anything except hands above)

10. Four cards to a straight—outside draw…draw one card *(break anything except hands above)*

11. Two cards to a royal flush with a jack or queen high …draw three cards *(break anything except hands above)*

12. Three cards to a one-deuce straight flush—double inside draw…draw two cards *(break anything except hands above)*

13. Four cards to a one-deuce straight—inside draw…draw one card

14. All other hands…discard and draw five cards

Deuce Hands

1. All pat hands…stand

2. Three deuces and two garbage cards…draw two cards

3. Four of a kind with one or two deuces…draw one card

4. Four cards to a royal flush with one or two deuces…draw one card *(break anything except hands above)*

5. Two deuces and three garbage cards…draw three cards *(break anything except hands above)*

6. Four cards to a one-deuce straight flush…draw one card *(break anything except hands above)*

7. Three of a kind with one deuce…draw two cards

8. One deuce plus garbage…draw four cards

Deuces Wild Three of a Kind or Better: 17-10-4-3 Machines with 4,000 coins for Royal Flush 101.6% Payback

```
Royal Flush . . . . . . . . . . . . . . . . . . . . . . . 800
Four Deuces . . . . . . . . . . . . . . . . . . . . . 500
Deuces Royal Flush . . . . . . . . . . . . . . . . . . 25
Five of a Kind . . . . . . . . . . . . . . . . . . . . 17
Straight Flush . . . . . . . . . . . . . . . . . . . . 10
Four of a Kind  . . . . . . . . . . . . . . . . . . . . 4
Full House  . . . . . . . . . . . . . . . . . . . . . . 3
Flush . . . . . . . . . . . . . . . . . . . . . . . . . . 2
Straight . . . . . . . . . . . . . . . . . . . . . . . . 2
Three of a Kind  . . . . . . . . . . . . . . . . . . . . 1
```

Strategy for Deuces Wild 17-10-4-3 Machines

Non-Deuce Hands

1. All pat hands ...stand

2. Four cards to a royal flush...draw one card (*break anything including a straight, flush, or a straight flush*)

3. Four of a kind...draw one card

4. Four cards to a straight flush—inside or outside draw ...draw one card (*break anything except hands above*)

5. Three of a kind...draw two cards

6. Three cards to a royal flush...draw two cards (*break anything except hands above*)

7. Three cards to a straight flush—inside or outside draw ...draw two cards (*break anything except hands above*)

8. Four cards to a flush...draw one card (*break anything except hands above*)

9. One pair...draw three cards (*break anything except hands above*)

10. Four cards to a straight …draw one card *(break anything except hands above)*

11. Two cards to a royal flush with a jack or queen high…draw three cards *(break anything except hands above)*

12. All other hands…discard and draw five cards

Deuce Hands

1. All pat hands…stand

2. Three deuces and two garbage cards…draw two cards

3. Four of a kind with one or two deuces…draw one card

4. Four cards to a royal with one or two deuces…draw one card *(break anything except hands above)*

5. Two deuces and three garbage cards…draw three cards *(break anything except hands above)*

6. Four cards to a one-deuce straight flush…draw one card *(break anything except hands above)*

7. Three of a kind with one deuce…draw two cards

8. Three cards to a one-deuce royal flush…draw two cards *(break anything except hands above)*

9. One deuce plus garbage…draw four cards

*Deuces Wild Three of a Kind or Better: 15-9-4-3 Machines with Progressive Jackpot for Royal Flush 100%+ Payback**

Royal Flush . . . . *Progressive
Four Deuces 200
Deuces Royal Flush 25
Five of a Kind 15
Straight Flush 9
Four of a Kind 4
Full House 3
Flush 2
Straight 2
Three of a Kind 1

(*Progressive jackpot must be at the following minimum levels for 100% payback: Nickels—$800; Quarters—$4,000; Dollars—$16,000.)

Strategy for Deuces Wild 15-9-4-3 Machines

Non-Deuce Hands

1. All pat hands …stand

2. Four cards to a royal flush…draw one card *(break anything including a straight, flush, or a straight flush)*

3. Four of a kind…draw one card

4. Three cards to a royal flush…draw two cards *(break anything except hands above)*

5. Three of a kind…draw two cards

6. Four cards to a straight flush—inside or outside draw…draw one card *(break anything except hands above)*

7. One pair…draw three cards *(break anything except hands above)*

8. Four cards to a straight...draw one card *(break anything except hands above)*

9. Four cards to a flush...draw one card *(break anything except hands above)*

10. Two cards to a royal flush ...draw three cards *(break anything except hands above)*

11. Three cards to a straight flush—inside or outside draw...draw two cards *(break anything except hands above)*

12. All other hands...discard and draw five cards

Deuce Hands

1. All pat hands...stand

2. Three deuces and two garbage cards...draw two cards

3. Four of a kind with one or two deuces...draw one card

4. Four cards to a royal with one or two deuces...draw one card *(break anything except hands above)*

5. Two deuces and three garbage cards...draw three cards *(break anything except hands above)*

6. Four cards to a one-deuce straight flush...draw one card *(break anything except hands above)*

7. Three of a kind with one deuce...draw two cards

8. Three cards to a one-deuce royal flush...draw two cards *(break anything except hands above)*

9. One deuce plus garbage...draw four cards

Play These Machines If You Must Deuces Wild Video Poker with 95% to 97.9% Return

Deuces Wild 10-8-4-4 Machines with 4,000 coins for Royal Flush 96% Payback

Royal Flush 800
Four Deuces 200
Deuces Royal Flush 20
Five of a Kind 10
Straight Flush 8
Four of a Kind 4
Full House 4
Flush 3
Straight 2
Three of a Kind 1

Strategy for Deuces Wild 10-8-4-4 Machines

Non-Deuce Hands

1. All pat hands …stand

2. Four cards to a royal flush…draw one card *(break anything including a straight, flush, or a straight flush)*

3. Four of a kind…draw one card

4. Three of a kind…draw two cards

5. Four cards to a straight flush—inside or outside draw…draw one card *(break anything except hands above)*

6. Three cards to a royal flush…draw two cards *(break anything except hands above)*

7. Four cards to a flush…draw one card *(break anything except hands above)*

8. One pair or two pairs…draw four or three three cards *(break anything except hands above)*

9. Four cards to a straight…draw one card *(break anything except hands above)*

10. Three cards to a straight flush—inside or outside draw…draw two cards *(break anything except hands above)*

11. Four cards to a straight—inside draw…draw one card *(break anything except hands above)*

12. Two cards to a royal flush…draw three cards *(break anything except hands above)*

12. All other hands…discard and draw five cards

Deuce Hands

1. All pat hands…stand

2. Three deuces and two garbage cards…draw two cards

3. Four of a kind with one or two deuces…draw one card

4. Four cards to a royal with one or two deuces…draw one card *(break anything except hands above)*

5. Two deuces and three garbage cards…draw three cards *(break anything except hands above)*

6. Four cards to a one-deuce straight flush—inside or outside draw…draw one card *(break anything except hands above)*

7. Three of a kind with one deuce…draw two cards

8. Three cards to a one-deuce royal flush…draw two cards *(break anything except hands above)*

9. One deuce plus garbage…draw four cards

Deuces Wild 16-13-4-3 Machines with 4,000 coins for Royal Flush 96.8% Payback

Royal Flush 800
Four Deuces 200
Deuces Royal Flush 25
Five of a Kind 16
Straight Flush 13
Four of a Kind 4
Full House 3
Flush 2
Straight 2
Three of a Kind 1

Strategy for Deuces Wild 16-13-4-3 Machines

Non-Deuce Hands

1. All pat hands…stand

2. Four cards to a royal flush…draw one card *(break anything including a straight, flush, or a straight flush)*

3. Four of a kind…draw one card

4. Three of a kind…draw two cards

5. Four cards to a straight flush—inside or outside draw …draw one card *(break anything except hands above)*

6. Three cards to a royal flush…draw two cards *(break anything except hands above)*

7. Three cards to a straight flush—outside draw…draw two cards *(break anything except hands above)*

8. Four cards to a flush…draw one card *(break anything except hands above)*

9. One pair…draw four or three three cards *(break anything except hands above)*

10. Four cards to a straight—outside draw...draw one card *(break anything except hands above)*

11. Two cards to a royal flush without an ace...draw three cards *(break anything except hands above)*

12. Three cards to a straight flush—inside draw...draw two cards

12. All other hands...discard and draw five cards

Deuce Hands

1. All pat hands...stand

2. Three deuces and two garbage cards...draw two cards

3. Four of a kind with one or two deuces...draw one card

4. Four cards to a royal with one or two deuces...draw one card *(break anything except hands above)*

5. Four cards to a one or two deuce straight flush—inside or outside draw...draw one card *(break anything except hands above)*

6. Two deuces and three garbage cards...draw three cards *(break anything except hands above)*

7. Three of a kind with one deuce...draw two cards

8. Three cards to a one-deuce royal flush...draw two cards *(break anything except hands above)*

9. One deuce plus garbage...draw four cards

Don't Play These Machines Deuces Wild Video Poker Machines With 94.9% or Less Return

Deuces Wild 18-8-4-3 Machines with 2,000 coins for Royal Flush 8 Coins for Maximum Play 94.6% Payback

Royal Flush 250
Four Deuces 250
Deuces Royal Flush 25
Five of a Kind 18
Straight Flush 8
Four of a Kind 4
Full House 3
Flush 2
Straight 2
Three of a Kind 1

Deuces Wild 15-11-4-3 Machines with 2,000 coins for Royal Flush 4 Coins for Maximum Play 92.9% Payback

Royal Flush 500
Four Deuces 100
Deuces Royal Flush 25
Five of a Kind 15
Straight Flush 11
Four of a Kind 4
Full House 3
Flush 2
Straight 2
Three of a Kind 1

Deuces Wild 20-10-4-3 Machines with 2,000 coins for Royal Flush 8 Coins for Maximum Play 94.7% Payback

Royal Flush 250
Four Deuces 200
Deuces Royal Flush 30
Five of a Kind 20
Straight Flush 10
Four of a Kind 4
Full House 3
Flush 2
Straight 2
Three of a Kind 1

Deuces Wild 15-11-4-3 Machines with 2,000 coins for Royal Flush 94.5% Payback

Royal Flush 400
Four Deuces 200
Deuces Royal Flush 25
Five of a Kind 15
Straight Flush 11
Four of a Kind 4
Full House 3
Flush 2
Straight 2
Three of a Kind 1

Deuces Wild 15-9-4-3 Machines with 4,000 coins for Royal Flush 94.3% Payback

Royal Flush 800
Four Deuces 200
Deuces Royal Flush 25
Five of a Kind 15
Straight Flush 9
Four of a Kind 4
Full House 3
Flush 2
Straight 2
Three of a Kind 1

Deuces Wild 10-8-4-4 Machines with 4,000 coins for Royal Flush 94% Payback

```
Royal Flush . . . . . . . . . . . . . . . . . . . . . . . 800
Four Deuces . . . . . . . . . . . . . . . . . . . . . . 200
Deuces Royal Flush . . . . . . . . . . . . . . . . . . 20
Five of a Kind . . . . . . . . . . . . . . . . . . . . . . 10
Straight Flush . . . . . . . . . . . . . . . . . . . . . . . 8
Four of a Kind  . . . . . . . . . . . . . . . . . . . . . . 4
Full House  . . . . . . . . . . . . . . . . . . . . . . . . 4
Flush  . . . . . . . . . . . . . . . . . . . . . . . . . . . . 2
Straight  . . . . . . . . . . . . . . . . . . . . . . . . . . 2
Three of a Kind  . . . . . . . . . . . . . . . . . . . . . 1
```

6

Victory at Tens or Better, other Video-Poker Versions and Novelty Games

There was a time when Tens-or-Better video poker was the biggest thing around. Well, it's still big in one sense because quite a few Tens-or-Better machines come in the Big Bertha variety. And Big Berthas are nothing if not BIG. Unfortunately, as the dinosaurs found out to their "neverlasting" chagrin, being big isn't necessarily a guarantee that you'll survive the ravages of time. Thus, even as I write this, many of the Tens-or-Better machines might be on the verge of extinction.

However, video poker is nothing if not faddish, and it's anyone's guess if seven or eight years from now the Tens-or-Better variety of video poker makes a remarkable comeback. If so, you'll be armed with a strong strategy as these machines will quite often offer great odds. Again, of course, you must study the face of this monster to figure out just what kind of beast it is. While many Tens-or-Better machines are great bets, others number among the worst creatures in video pokerland. Beware.

This chapter will be arranged according to the playability of the various machines, starting with the good bets—those machines that are paying back 98% or more.

Tens or Better: 6-5-4-3 Video Poker with 4,000 coins for Royal Flush 99.1% Payback

Royal Flush 800
Straight Flush 50
Four of a Kind 25
Full House 6
Flush 5
Straight 4
Three of a Kind 3
Two Pairs 2
Tens or Better 1

Strategy for Tens or Better

1. All pat hands...stand

2. Four cards to a royal flush...draw one card (*break anything including a flush or a straight*)

3. Three of a kind...draw two cards

4. Four cards to a straight flush—inside or outside draw ...draw one card (*break anything except hands above*)

5. Two pairs...draw one card

6. Tens or better...draw three cards (*break anything except hands above*)

7. Three cards to a royal flush...draw two cards (*break anything except hands above*)

8. Four cards to a flush...draw one card (*break anything except hands above*)

9. Four cards to a straight with a jack or queen or king high...draw one card (*break anything except hands above*)

10. Low pair…draw three cards *(break anything except hands above)*

11. Three cards to a straight flush with a ten or jack high— inside or outside draw…draw two cards *(break anything except hands above)*

12. Four cards to a straight…draw one card *(break anything except hands above)*

13. Two cards to a royal flush with jack, queen or king high…draw three cards *(break anything except hands above)*

14. Four cards to a straight with ace high—inside draw…draw one card *(break anything except hands above)*

15. Three cards to a straight flush—inside or outside draws …draw two cards *(break anything except hands above)*

16. One, two or three high cards…draw four, three cards or two cards

17. All other hands…discard and draw five cards

Two Pairs or Better: 12-8-6-3 Video Poker with 4,000 coins for Royal Flush 98% Payback

Royal Flush	800
Straight Flush	100
Four of a Kind	50
Full House	12
Flush	8
Straight	6
Three of a Kind	3
Two Pairs	2

Strategy for Two Pairs or Better

1. All pat hands…stand

2. Four cards to a royal flush…draw one card (*break anything including a straight or a flush*)

3. Four cards to a straight flush—outside draw…draw one card (*break anything except hands above*)

4. Three of a kind…draw two cards

5. Four cards to a straight flush—inside draw…draw one card (*break anything except hands above*)

6. Two pairs…draw one card

7. Four cards to a flush…draw one card (*break anything except hands above*)

8. Three cards to a royal flush…draw two cards (*break anything except hands above*)

9. Four cards to a straight—outside draw…draw one card (*break anything except hands above*)

10. Any pair…draw three cards (*break anything except hands above*)

11. Three cards to a straight flush—inside or outside draw …draw two cards (*break anything except hands above*)

12. Four cards to a straight—inside draw…draw one card (*break anything except hands above*)

13. Three cards to a flush…draw two cards (*break anything except hands above*)

14. Two cards to a royal flush…draw three cards (*break anything except hands above*)

15. Two cards to a straight flush…draw three cards (*break anything except hands above*)

16. Three cards to a straight…draw two cards (*break anything except hands above*)

17. One ten…draw four cards

18. One high card…draw four cards

19. All other hands…discard and draw five cards

Deuces and Joker Wild: 9-6-3-3 Video Poker with 10,000 coins for Five Wild Cards 99% Payback

Four Deuces and Joker 2,000
Natural Royal Flush 800
Four Deuces 25
Wild Royal Flush 12
Five of a Kind 9
Straight Flush 6
Four of a Kind 3
Full House 3
Flush 3
Straight 2
Three of a Kind 1

Strategy for Deuces and Joker Wild Video Poker

Non-Wild Card Hands

1. All pat hands…stand

2. Four cards to a royal flush…draw one card *(break anything including a straight, a flush or a straight flush)*

3. Four of a kind…draw one card

4. Three of a kind…draw two cards

5. Four cards to a straight flush—inside or outside draw …draw one card *(break anything except hands above)*

6. Three cards to a royal flush…draw two cards *(break anything except hands above)*

7. Four cards to a flush…draw one card *(break anything except hands above)*

8. Two pairs…draw one card

9. Three cards to a straight flush—inside or outside draws …draw two cards *(break anything except hands above)*

10. One pair…draw three cards *(break anything except hands above)*

11. Four cards to a straight—inside or outside draw…draw one card

12. All other hands…discard and draw five cards

Wild Card Hands

1. All pat hands…stand

2. Four deuces…draw one card

3. Three deuces and joker…draw one card

4. Three deuces plus garbage…draw two cards

5. Two deuces and joker plus garbage…draw two cards

6. Four of a kind with one or two wild cards…draw one card *(break anything except hands above)*

7. Four cards to a royal flush with one or two wild cards …draw one card *(break anything except hands above)*

8. Two deuces plus garbage…draw three cards *(break anything except hands above)*

9. One deuce and the joker plus garbage…draw three cards *(break anything except hands above)*

10. Four cards to a straight flush with one wild card…draw one card *(break anything except hands above)*

11. Three of a kind with one wild card…draw two cards *(break anything except hands above)*

12. Three cards to a royal flush with one wild card…draw two cards *(break anything except hands above)*

13. Four cards to a straight with one wild card…draw one card *(break anything except hands above)*

14. Four cards to a flush with one wild card…draw one card *(break anything except hands above)*

15. Three cards to a straight flush with one wild card…draw two cards *(break anything except hands above)*

16. One deuce or one joker plus garbage…draw four cards

Play If You Must Video Poker with 95% to 97.9% Return

Double Joker Two Pairs or Better Video Poker with 4,000 coins for Natural Royal Flush 97.7% Payback

Natural Royal Flush 800
Joker Royal Flush 100
Five of a Kind 50
Straight Flush. 25
Four of a Kind. 8
Full House 5
Flush 4
Straight 3
Three of a Kind 2
Two Pairs. 1

Strategy for Double Joker Poker Two Pairs or Better

Non Joker Hands

1. All pat hands…stand

2. Four cards to a royal flush…draw one card *(break anything including a straight or a flush)*

3. Four of a kind…draw one card

4. Three of a kind…draw two cards

5. Four cards to a straight flush—inside or outside draw …draw one card *(break anything except hands above)*

6. Two pairs…draw one card

7. Three cards to a royal flush…draw two cards *(break anything except hands above)*

8. Four cards to a flush...draw one card *(break anything except hands above)*

9. Any pair...draw three cards *(break anything except hands above)*

10. Three cards to a straight flush—inside or outside draw ...draw two cards *(break anything except hands above)*

11. Four cards to a straight—inside or outside draw...draw one card *(break anything except hands above)*

12. Two cards to a royal flush...draw three cards

13. All other hands...discard and draw five cards

Joker Hands

1. All pat hands...stand

2. Four of a kind with one or two jokers...draw one card

3. Four cards to a royal flush with one or two jokers...draw one card *(break anything including a joker straight or joker flush)*

4. Four cards to a straight flush with two jokers—inside or outside draw...draw one card *(break anything, including a joker straight or joker flush, except hands above)*

5. Three of a kind with one joker...draw two cards *(break anything except hands above)*

6. Two jokers plus garbage...draw three cards

7. Three cards to a royal with one joker...draw two cards *(break anything except hands above)*

8. Three or four cards to a straight flush with one joker— inside or outside draws...draw two or one card *(break anything except hands above)*

9. Four cards to a straight with one joker—inside or out-side draw...draw one card *(break anything except hands above)*

10. Four cards to a flush with one joker...draw one card *(break anything except hands above)*

11. One joker plus garbage...draw four cards

Don't Play These Machines Video Poker with 94.9% or Less Return

Tens or Better: 9-6-4-3 Video Poker with 4,000 coins for Royal Flush 90.8% Payback

```
Royal Flush . . . . . . . . . . . . . . . . . . . . . . . 800
Straight Flush . . . . . . . . . . . . . . . . . . . . . 50
Four of a Kind . . . . . . . . . . . . . . . . . . . . 25
Full House . . . . . . . . . . . . . . . . . . . . . . . 9
Flush . . . . . . . . . . . . . . . . . . . . . . . . . . . 6
Straight . . . . . . . . . . . . . . . . . . . . . . . . . 4
Three of a Kind . . . . . . . . . . . . . . . . . . . 3
Two Pairs . . . . . . . . . . . . . . . . . . . . . . . . 1
Tens or Better . . . . . . . . . . . . . . . . . . . . . 1
```

Tens or Better: 10-8-6-2 Video Poker with 2,400 coins for Royal Flush (8 coins for maximum pay) 92.4% Payback

```
Royal Flush . . . . . . . . . . . . . . . . . . . . . . 300
Straight Flush . . . . . . . . . . . . . . . . . . . . 150
Four of a Kind . . . . . . . . . . . . . . . . . . . . 30
Full House . . . . . . . . . . . . . . . . . . . . . . . 10
Flush . . . . . . . . . . . . . . . . . . . . . . . . . . . 8
Straight . . . . . . . . . . . . . . . . . . . . . . . . . 6
Three of a Kind . . . . . . . . . . . . . . . . . . . 2
Two Pairs . . . . . . . . . . . . . . . . . . . . . . . . 1
Tens or Better . . . . . . . . . . . . . . . . . . . . . 1
```

Kings or Better: 11-7-4-3 Video Poker with 2,000 coins for Royal Flush (8 coins for maximum pay) 94.7% Payback

Royal Flush 250
Straight Flush 195
Four of a Kind 22
Full House 11
Flush 7
Straight 4
Three of a Kind 3
Two Pairs 2
Kings or Better 1

Two Pairs or Better: 11-7-5-3 Video Poker with 5,000 coins for Royal Flush 94% Payback

Royal Flush 1,000
Straight Flush 100
Four of a Kind 50
Full House 11
Flush 7
Straight 5
Three of a Kind 3
Two Pairs 2

Deuces and Joker Wild: 12-7-3-2 Video Poker with 2,000 coins for Five Wild Cards (4 coins for maximum pay) 93% Payback

Four Deuces and Joker 500
Natural Royal Flush 400
Four Deuces 100
Wild Royal Flush 20
Five of a Kind 12
Straight Flush 7
Four of a Kind 3
Full House 2
Flush 2
Straight 1
Three of a Kind 1

Novelty Games

In the future this heading could be misleading. After all, what is a novelty game? My definition is something new, experimental or rare. By that definition all video-poker machines would have been novelty machines in the past. In fact, they were. Today, video poker is standard fare in casinos. However, right now, this minute, as I pen these words, the following machines are novelties because you won't find many of them around: Double-Card Poker, Second-Chance, and Double-Down Stud. Actually, that's good news because most versions are not great bets. The casinos have introduced many of these machines—indeed the casinos have introduced a host of variations for all standard video-poker fare—with bad intentions: to confuse the players sufficiently to wean them off the better-paying machines. They are giving you a multitude of games to choose from so that they can multiply *their* profits.

Double-Card Video Poker

This is a variation of Jacks-or-Better with a 53rd card added to the deck. While this card is not wild per se, it can be used to "enhance" certain hands. Thus, if you get this "double card" with a pair of jacks or better, two pairs, three-of-a-kind, or four-of-a-kind, you will be paid double on that hand. This is a sucker game because many poor hands that initially receive this "double card" will be played incorrectly. Instead of discarding the card, the player will hold it in the hopes of getting a pair to go with it. The best way to play this machine is to treat the "double card" as a garbage card on the initial round if it isn't already increasing the value of a pair of jacks or better. Actually, the very best way to play this game is to walk by it and double over with laughter.

Second-Chance Machines

The second-chance option at first sounds like a good deal. You have the right to place a second wager and receive a second draw if that draw could result in a hand that is a straight or better. In all novelty games with a second-chance option, you simply ask yourself this question: Is the original version of the game—that is, the game with no second-chance feature—any good? If the answer is yes, then the second-chance option, although risking more money, will also be good—provided nothing has been changed on the original payout. This, unfortunately, is usually not the case. So if you find your favorite machine having this second-chance option, check it very carefully to make sure that none of the other payouts have been altered. The least alteration in a payout will throw the game into a bad bet for you.

Double Down Stud

This machine game is a take-off on the table game of the same name. It's a simple game to play because you really don't have many choices to make. It's not such an horrendous bet, either, because the house has an approximately 2.5% edge.

The dealer-in-the-machine deals you four cards. Now, you can decide whether to double your initial bet before receiving a fifth card. Still, with the variety of machines out there, your best bet is to pass this stud by.

Pay Schedule

(Based on maximum coin play)
Royal Flush 2,000
Straight Flush 200
Four of a Kind 50
Full House 12
Flush 9
Straight 6
Three of a Kind 4
Two Pair 3
Pair of Jacks—Aces 2
Pair of sixes—10's 1

The strategy for Double Down Stud is rather simple. Obviously, it's in your interest to double your bet anytime you have a paying hand. You would also double your bet on any possible flush or any possible straight with an outside draw.

How to Play Low-Paying Video-Poker Machines

This is not a real chapter but...a RESPITE from serious considerations of strategy

There are two simple and fun strategies you can employ for the low-paying machines I've alerted you to in the preceding chapters, those in the under 94.9% category—strategies that are wonderful to play if you are sadistically inclined and lacking in any human decency, that is. Also if you are not afraid to be killed or maimed.

Take a bucket of coins and go to a machine in an area with very little traffic. Make sure no one is playing any machines near you. Now, take heaping handfuls of coin and dump them into the tray—dump them as hard and loud as you can. With each dump, let out a scream: "Hooray! Another winner!" When people come over—as they inevitably will, jump up and down and shout: "I know these machines are supposed to stink but, hell, I've been winning a fortune on them! Yahoo!" Now, scoop up all the coins and put them back into your bucket stating for all to hear: "God, looks like this machine could hit forever!" For those of you who are really devious and have not the slightest drop of the milk

149

of human kindness in your heart, turn to the assembled crowd and offer to sell the machine to them. "Hey, for twenty bucks, I'll let you have the machine because I gotta go. Anyone interested?" You might even be able to start a bidding war.

For Joker Poker you can follow a specific strategy. Since you are dealing with machines that have a joker, you will become a human joker. In this way you can maximize your chance of actually turning a rather large negative expectation into a decidedly positive one—or die trying.

Here's what you do.

Go to the area of the casino where the lowest-paying joker-poker machines can be found (in some states, notably New Jersey and Louisiana, this will be the entire casino because all the joker-poker varieties are low paying). Then start telling really stupid jokes. You might want to purchase a book or two of stupid jokes and just read them at the top of your lungs. Laugh heartily at every awful joke you make. Or, get some really funny jokes and butcher them. Tell them so badly that people can't follow the punchline even if they are trying to follow the joke. You might even want to dress up like a court jester to really solidify the effect.

Now, three things will probably happen to you after a short while of this behavior: the security guards will escort you out of the casino, or several patrons will pay you to leave the area, or an enraged patron will kill you. If the second in the foregoing sequence happens, you will have made money. If the third happens, your heirs will have made money (if you have insurance). If the first happens, consider it a push.

[My wife and gaming partner, the beautiful A.P., informs me that many readers don't want to read my adolescent humor concerning what to do with low-paying machines. What she doesn't realize is that having researched, analyzed, and written the strategies for the good versions of the machines contained in the first six chapters of this book, I'm drunk on statistics and computer programs and I have a sneaky feeling that my computer monitor is sending me signals from aliens in space. These signals said: "Take a break, take a break, before plunging on." So who should I listen to? My wife? Or superior beings from the planet V.D.O. who are speaking to me through my monitor?]

The respite is over. We plunge onward.

7

Money Management and the Mental Edge Redux

In regular poker when you're going head to head with a human opponent, it is not difficult to understand how easy it is for a player to be "psyched out." The other player's supposedly superior skill, his panache, his past playing decisions can all lead an opponent to the edge of the abyss—thus becoming "psyched out." "Psyched out" can be defined by a whole host of phrases and clichés (all of them right on the button). Being "psyched out" is the losing of one's rhythm, confidence, judgment, or optimism in the face of a seemingly superior opponent. It's been alternately called "freezing" in sports contests and "going on tilt" in gambling games. For college students (or any students), being "psyched out" means being "out of it" on a test. ("Damn, Professor, I knew the answers, I just couldn't remember them. I was out of it.") To some degree, all of us have probably experienced the phenomena of being "psyched out" at one time or another in our lives. Some of us have also experienced, and perhaps enjoyed, the phenomenon of psyching someone else out. When you're psyched out, you are the deer in the head-lights of a car—frozen and doomed. When you're doing the psyching, however, you are an eighteen-wheeler barrelling down on Bambi.

Can one be psyched out by a machine? Definitely yes. I'd call this situation self-psyching out, because the player would do it to himself. Since I love inventing psychobabble, let's call this the Self-Psyching-Out Syndrome! (Or SOS—we'll drop the "P.")

How would the SOS manifest itself? I believe that if a player is psyched out it will usually show in how he manages his money and the types of bets he makes. However, a player could play perfectly and still be psyched out. There comes a time in every losing session where you have to say to yourself: "Am I done for the day? Have I lost all I can afford or want to lose for this session?" No matter how often an individual gam-bles, it feels bad to lose. But a person who is psyched out almost wants to lose—that's the strange thing. It's almost as if at a certain point the object of the player's desire is no longer beating the casino but beating himself. Suddenly the player takes a perverse joy in inflicting more punishment upon him-self, like the boxer who punches himself in the face because his opponent just got through his guard and punched him in his face. It's a double dose of indignity.

And video poker can certainly set up the necessary condi-tions for a player to be psyched out. Most video-poker games have long losing streaks and most sessions will be losers. That fact should not make you believe that you are doomed to lose—that you deserve to lose; that somehow or other you have been a bad little boy or girl and must be punished for it. Yet I've seen people behave this way. Remember that you are play-ing the best video-poker games because you want to win money. Why else would you have bought this book? The fact that you intellectually know that more often than not you will lose should not predispose you to taking those losses lightly or, conversely, to heart. Never get to the point where you say to yourself: "Screw it! I'll keep playing until I lose all the money I brought." Get into that frame of mind and you could lose your entire stake in one unlucky session. On some nights Lady Luck is no lady but a cheap whore who will give her favors to the house. Walk away from her.

I have mentioned it on numerous occasions in this book but it bears repeating once more: video poker is volatile. You will have explosive winning sessions and many grinding losing sessions. So you must play a contained game and stay on top of yourself. Although your opponent is only a machine, it is a machine that is incapable of psyching itself out or of being psyched out. The dealer-in-the-machine will deal, collect, and deal some more—deal, collect, and deal some more—until the edge of doom. Just don't let that doom be yours.

The Importance of Comps

I have thoroughly covered both the psychology of comps and the way casinos figure the value of your play in my book *Guerrilla Gambling: How to Beat the Casinos at Their Own Games!* I have also discussed how to get more comps than your play actually warrants in that book. Suffice it to say that you should never play just to get comps. However, you should always take whatever comps your play warrants. For many astute gamblers, the combination of comps and play will equal long-term success. Always put your comp card in the machine when you play or give it into the change person to record your buy-in.

To give you some idea of the streaky nature of video poker and also how comps can help offset otherwise losing trips, the following is a day-by-day Las Vegas diary of mine that shows 28 straight days of playing Jacks-or-Better 9/6 video poker with 4,700 coins for the royal flush. Every morning I played the same good video-poker machine for $500 (five quarters per hand = 400 hands per day = 11,200 hands = $14,000 through the machine during the 28 day period). When I was finished playing on a given day I would ask for a comp for breakfast. The amount of the comp shown on this chart is what I actually spent as opposed to what I theoretically could have spent. Since I don't make a pig of myself, I only ordered what I would have ordered had I paid for the meal myself.

Day	Won	Lost	Comp Amount	Total
1		$34	$14	- $20.00
2	$17.50		$21	+ $38.50
3	$27.50		$18	+ $45.50
4		$10	$16.82	+ $6.82
5		$10	$14.86	+ 4.86
6		$26	$8.45	- $17.55
7	$12		$18.45	+ $30.45
8		$73	$8.45	- $64.55
9		$72.50	$14.86	- $57.64
10	$84		$14.75	+ $98.75
11		$109	$8.45	- $100.55
12		$74.25	$18	- $56.25
13	$33		$8.45	+ $41.45
14	$58.50		$21.35	+ $79.85
15	$5		$8.45	+ $13.45
16	$33		$18.45	+ $51.45
17		$91.50	$8.45	- $83.05
18		$200	$18	- $182
19		$20	$18	- $2.00
20		$68	$8.45	- $59.55
21	$20		$21	+ $41.00
22		$34	$8.45	- $25.55
23	$134		$14.25	+ $148.25
24	$35		$8.45	+ $33.45
25	$62		$14.86	+ $76.86
26		$34.50	$8.45	- $26.05
27	$17.25		$21	+ $38.25
28		$62.50	$8.45	- $54.05
Totals	$538.75	$919.25	$390.60	+ $10.10

Although I had no truly awesome days during this 28-day playing cycle (I never received a straight flush, for example, and never got close to a royal flush), the combination of comps and play netted me $10.10. Now, at first glance this $10.10 win might seem nothing to gloat about…but think again. A win is a win, after all. Had I not played video poker in this particular casino every morning, I would have had to pay $390.60 for my breakfasts over this period of time. Instead, the casino gave me $10.10 to eat for 28 days in their restaurant. Looked at that way—I received some bargain.

Money Management

The writer of the biblical book Ecclesiastes remarks that "there is nothing new under the sun." He could have just as easily been putting pen to paper and writing this section. The money management advice I'm about to give has been given before by me and hundreds of other gambling writers before me.

First and foremost, only play with money that has been specifically set aside for the purposes of gambling. I do this by having a separate checking account that has only my gambling stake in it. I originally built my initial stake by slating the fees from extra writing jobs just for gambling. At a certain point I had what I wanted in that account and I was ready to begin my career as a gambler. Now, I take my markers out against this account and play only a small percentage of the account on any given day. If the account goes over a certain total amount, I take the excess and use it for other purposes. When the total goes under a certain amount, I adjust how much I will allot for my individual sessions and how much I'll bet at any given time. In this way, I assure myself of enough of a bankroll to weather the very worst losing streaks. This method of cost accounting has served me well.

Okay, with cliché paragraph duly noted, what should you consider a sizable enough bankroll to engage Lady Luck at video poker? Instead of using dollar amounts, let's talk in terms of coins. A coin will be defined as the single-coin amount of your machine. If you are playing a 25-cent machine, then 25 cents is one coin. If you are playing a dollar machine, then a dollar is one coin. Since you will always be playing maximum coin, it will usually cost you five coins for one hand of video poker. (Some machines do take four coins, some eight or more, as the maximum. You'll have to adjust accordingly.)

Ask yourself the question: How long do I want to play? Or, how many shots at Lady Luck do I want to take?

Let us say you want to play for four hours a day for three days. That's 12 hours of total play. Assuming four hands a minute (one hand every 15 seconds—a rather moderate pace), you would play 2,880 hands of video poker in that three-day period.

Now, you have a choice to make. Do you play any credits during your sessions or do you stick to playing coins? Persona

I never play any credits. I put my money through the machine once and once only. Thus, facing a three-day, 12 hour, 2,880 hand assault on Lady Luck, I would need 14,400 coins (2,880 hands × 5 coins = 14,400 coins). So does that mean that if I wanted to play a dollar machine, I would need $14,400 behind me? Not really.

Just take one day, which would be 4800 coins ($4,800 dollars for dollar machines, $1,200 for quarter machines, and $240 for nickel machines) and make that your trip-stake. This is the money you are going to risk. You will put the money through the machine that first day—once. However, do not put all your coins into the machine during one session. Instead, divide the day into two or more sessions and allot the requisite amount for each. Only play the money originally slated for each session and never play credits. If you wind up with more than 4,800 coins at the end of the first day, the excess is put away, not to be touched on this trip. That excess will go back into your gambling account when you get home.

The second day, you would again put 4,800 coins through the machine—just once—and again spread out the play amongst various sessions. On the third day, same procedure. Should your trip bankroll fall below 4,800 coins at any time, you would risk whatever you had by putting it through the machine once. So, on that first day, let us say that you took a beating and lost half your stake—a not impossible occurrence. On day two, you would put through 2,400 coins because that's all you had left. And you would put them through during individual sessions, not all at once. You would have to cut down the length and/or number of sessions because of your shortened bankroll.

Using this method of play, it is impossible for you to lose every penny unless the unthinkable happens—every day is a losing day and you lose every single hand on the last day of your trip. If this horrible fate happens, you could still make money by selling your story (MEET THE UNLUCKIEST PERSON ON EARTH!) to the *Guinness Book of World Records or Ripley's Believe It or Not!*

While four hours a day of playing video poker might seem like a lot, it really isn't. Many video-poker aficionados will play six, eight, ten or more hours a day—as the last chapter of this book will show. If you are the type who wishes to put in mega-time at video poker, then you must adjust your bankroll accordingly.

Here's the best formula for figuring out what you need (if you use my preferred playing method above): total hours allotted for play per day × the number of days × number of hands per minute × 60 minutes × 5 coins = total coins necessary. Now, take that figure and divide by three. This is the amount of money you will need to bring to the casino. If you are playing at a machine that requires more or fewer than five coins, just adjust that last section to reflect this.

For extended trips, you might want to increase by a factor of two the total amount you bring with you—just to feel safe. Thus, if you are going to be staying in a casino town for six days, you might want to bring twice as much as you would for a three-day stake. In this way, you can assure yourself of the best shot at Lady Luck without your bankroll being plugged full of holes. There's no worse feeling than going away to a casino town for a week or more and being down most of your bankroll in the first few days.

In truth, the bottom line in the money-management, mental-edge, how-much-do-I-play-with sweepstakes is you. Some individuals can stand a high danger quotient. They can play with money that is not specifically set aside for gambling and break nary a sweat. (I am not referring to problem or compulsive gamblers whose whole lives revolve around sweat—and often blood and more often tears.) Other gamblers are much more timid. I'm in that category. I have friends who are the devil-may-care type but I'm one of the angels who do care. Thus, my advice is always conservative and, yes, perhaps at times a little timid. So be it. Yet, I do know this: playing as I've outlined above gives you a good chance of winning in the long run and an almost perfect chance of never losing it all in one orgy of bad luck. So play the best machines with the best strategies and give yourself plenty of money to play with and you will have the best chance for victory at video poker.

8

Victory at Video Blackjack

Blackjack or "21" is without a doubt the most popular table game in American casinos today. Part of the reason for its popularity is the fact that it is a game that can be beaten theoretically by skilled players. In addition, it is a game of choices. The player is actively involved with the results of his play. This combination of skill, choice and luck has caused a blackjack explosion in this country ever since Edward O. Thorp published his seminal work, *Beat the Dealer*, in the 1960's.

On the flip side, blackjack is the biggest money maker of all the table games for the casinos. Despite the fact that skillful players can beat it, more unskilled or semi-skilled players play the game than do skillful ones. For every card counter who can scratch out a 0.5 to 1.5 percent edge, there are hundreds, if not thousands, of uninformed, unskilled players giving the casinos edges of 2.5 to eight percent or more. Why these players persist on playing versions of "I have my own strategy" is beyond me; especially when great blackjack books are available for novice players, such as *Julian's No-Nonsense Guide to Winning Blackjack* by John F. Julian. These books can teach anyone of average intelligence how to cut the casino's edge to a minimum and, in some cases, get the edge for themselves. With a little effort, very little effort, anyone can become a good blackjack player. Yet, strangely, poor players and poor play abound. It's almost as if people don't want to win.

The video versions of blackjack share with their table-game cousin certain family traits. Thus, if you've played the table-game of blackjack, you will be familiar with the basic procedures of the machine variety. Most good video-blackjack games will allow doubling down on any first two cards, splitting pairs, doubling after splits, insurance, and some machines will even allow surrender. Like the table game of blackjack, there are video-blackjack games where the player can get an edge—in fact, some machines are so liberal that a skillful card counter (yes, you can count cards at video blackjack) can attain edges of over two percent!

As in the table game of blackjack, not all video-blackjack games are alike. There are better and worse games. How does one determine which is which? Just as you would in regular blackjack—the rules and options and paybacks must be analyzed.

If you are a blackjack player, you might be asking yourself why bother playing the machine variety? There are quite a few incentives for playing the machine version as opposed to the table version. The first, and most obvious, is that the machine version is cheaper. Most games will allow anywhere from one to 10 quarters or from one to 10 dollars to be wagered on a given round. Contrast this with the table game limits. Many casinos in America and around the world have very high minimum bet requirements for playing the table games. For example, in Atlantic City on weekends most table blackjack games will have minimums of $10, $15 and $25. Just one table-game bet could be your whole stake on a video-blackjack game!

A second, and quite compelling, reason to consider video blackjack concerns the casinos' response to expert play. They do nothing. That's right, you can play unmolested. Unlike a card counter at regular blackjack, the card counter at video blackjack doesn't have to worry about being banned, shuffled up on, or in any way harassed because of his skill. It's stress free. Or, at least, the only stress is whether you win or lose. In the table game variety, how you play the game can cause expert players more stress than winning or losing. Just experience being asked to leave a casino "because you're too good" and you'll know what I mean. Not so with video blackjack. The same casino-executive yabboes who flock to the table pits at the first indication of skillful play and who make life miserable for the card counter will smile pleasantly at the video-blackjack patron and then ignore him. Utterly.

The third reason for considering play at video blackjack is the same rational for playing at video poker. You can play your game without having to deal with other players and dealers. It's just you, the dealer-in-the-machine, and the gods of chance. It's a solitary contest played out in private.

However, before getting to the nitty-gritty of percentages and playing strategies for video blackjack, a little refresher course is in order. If you have never played the game, it is important to understand the sequences of decision making and the various options available to you.

In most of the newer versions of video-blackjack, you are given a set time limit in which to make your decision (usually six to 10 seconds) at which point the machine will lock in your initial two-card hand. This is where video blackjack will depart from video poker—the machine sets the playing pace in many video-blackjack games. However, you will also find machines that do not set a time limit for decision making. These will allow you to play at your own pace.

How Video Blackjack is Played

Blackjack appears to be a simple game and, indeed, its structure is quite easy to follow. All the cards have their face value. An eight equals an eight, a two equals a two, and so forth. All picture cards equal 10 as does, naturally, a 10. An ace equals either an 11 or a one. It is up to the player to decide how he is using the ace. Hands with an ace as one of the first two cards are called *soft hands*. Hands without an ace as one of the first two cards are called *hard hands*.

The objective of a blackjack game is to beat the dealer or, in video-blackjack terms, the dealer-in-the-machine. This can be done in one of two ways. You can beat the dealer because you have a better hand or you can beat the dealer because he has gone over 21 and *busted*. If either the player or the dealer has an ace and a 10 value card as his first two cards, this is called a blackjack or *natural* and is usually paid off at three to two (or 1.5 to one) for the player in the table-game version. However, many of the video-poker games you'll find will pay two *for* one. This is not as good as it sounds because two for one merely means an even money bet. You are getting back your one-unit bet and your one-unit win; thus two for one. In a three to two payoff, you are actually receiving 2.5 units in return for a one unit bet: your initial one-unit bet and your 1.5-unit win. Paying this way gives the casino a hefty edge over the player, as you shall see in the chart "Rule Changes and Their Effects on the Player's Edge." This hefty edge can only be equalized if the machine has extraordinary payouts for other types of hands—a rarity indeed.

If the dealer has a blackjack and the player has a blackjack, the hand is a standoff or *push* and nobody wins. In fact, any time the dealer and the player have the same valued hand it is a *push*. Never play in a blackjack game where the dealer wins the pushes, unless it is a face-up or double exposure game, the strategy for which is quite different than for regular blackjack. In video poker, you will find some machines where the house takes the pushes. Avoid these like the plague.

Blackjack tables generally seat six to seven players but video blackjack is usually a head to head affair, player vs. dealer-in-the-machine. However, newer versions of video blackjack will have the capacity to deal to as many as four players per round. This is an ideal game for card counters—especially if you are given more than one round before the dealer-in-the-machine shuffles up.

When you put your coins in, the dealer-in-the-machine will deal you two cards face up. The dealer-in-the-machine also deals himself two cards, one face up and one face down. All your playing decisions will be based on the face-up card of the dealer-in-the-machine.

Once the player is dealt his first two cards, he must decide whether to ask the dealer-in-the-machine to *hit* him, that is, give him another card; or, he must indicate that he is content with his first two cards and will *stand*.

The player can also decide to do any of the following:

1. If he has a pair of the same number, the player can *split* them and make each card the first card of a new hand. The dealer will then deal him a second card on the first hand and the player will play out that hand. When he is finished, the dealer will deal him a second card on the second hand and the player will play out that one.

2. The player can *double down* on his first two cards (when allowed). This means that the player is placing a bet equal to or less than his initial bet and will now receive only one card.

3. In some video-blackjack games, the player can *surrender* his hand. That means he gives up playing the hand in exchange for losing only half his bet.

4. The player can *insure* his hand against a dealer's face-up ace. He would put in a bet that can be as much as half his original bet. The insurance bet pays two to one. This bet is a side bet where the player who is insuring is wagering that the dealer-in-the-machine indeed has a blackjack—thus, the dealer-in-the-machine has a 10 in the hole with the ace on top. This is a very poor bet and should never be made, unless the player is counting cards and has a reasonable assurance that the 10 is underneath.

If the player should bust his hand (go over 21), the dealer-in-the-machine will immediately indicate that this round is over. In a game with more than one player, if the dealer-in-the-machine should subsequently bust, the player who has busted first still loses. This is the casino's biggest edge—the player must play his hand first and if he busts, regardless of what the dealer-in-the-machine does, the player loses.

Once the player(s) has played his hand(s), the dealer-in-the-machine plays his. However, the dealer-in-the-machine does not have any individual discretion in the playing of the hands but must play according to a prearranged set of rules. These rules are usually posted on the machine or can be found by pushing the INFORMATION button on the console. There is very little variation from machine to machine. The dealer-in-the-machine must hit all hands that total 16 or less, and stand on all hands that total 17 or more. The only area where machines differ in the application of these rules concerns the soft hand of 17 (ace + six). Some machines have their dealers-in-the-machine stand on soft 17. Some machines have their dealers-in-the-machine hit a soft 17. It is to the player's advantage if the dealer-in-the-machine stands on a soft 17.

When the dealer-in-the-machine has finished playing his hand, he pays off and/or takes the bets from the losers who didn't bust beforehand.

Simple? Quite. Yet, there are many rules variations within the structure of blackjack that can make the game more or less favorable for the players.

Blackjack Rules and Their Effect on the Player's Edge

There are good video-blackjack games and bad video-blackjack games and you should be able to distinguish between them. Basic strategy players and card counters alike benefit by liberal rules and are hurt by tight games with few options for the players. Even if the option is only marginally helpful to a player, it is better to play at a machine with this option, all other things being equal. The world of video blackjack is an ever-changing landscape and new rules come and go. However, for good or ill, most of the following rules can be found often enough in machines that it is worth knowing their impact on your expectations. Some of these variations are not yet found in video blackjack but more than likely will be in the near future—so forewarned is forearmed.

What follows will first be a discussion of the rule or option, followed by its percentage impact on the game. The percentages were prepared and furnished by John F. Julian, author of *Julian's No-Nonsense Guide to Winning Blackjack* and *The Julian Strategies in Roulette*.

All these percentages are based on a comparison of their impact on a single-deck game with Las Vegas Strip rules. This will be our model. The rules for the Las Vegas single-deck game are as follows: a player can double on any first two cards; player can split any pairs and double after splits. Blackjack pays three to two and insurance is allowed. This game is effectively even. In video-poker terms it is a 100 percent payback game. A double-deck game with the same rules favors the house by 0.35 percent. In video-blackjack parlance that machine is a 99.65 percent payback game. Percentages are based on playing perfect basic strategy.

Doubling on any first two cards

A good rule for the basic strategy player when used properly. For basic strategy players, follow the doubling strategies for the single and/or multiple decks as detailed later in this chapter. For the card counter, this is an even better rule since a card counter will find many more opportunities upon which to double. If the dealer-in-the-machine should have a blackjack, you only lose your initial bet on any double down. (No percentage value since this is part of the above 100 percent machine model.)

Doubling on 9, 10, and 11 only

This is not a good rule for single deck basic strategy players since there are times when you will want to double on eight. This rule is primarily aimed, however, against card counters to diminish their opportunities for doubling in advantageous situations. Value: -0.13 percent.

Doubling on 10 and 11 only

Awful rule and any game that stipulates this should be avoided if better games are available. Value: -0.28 percent.

Doubling on 11 only

Yuck. Value: -0.78 percent.

Splitting Aces

Good rule, especially if the machine allows you to resplit aces. When you split aces you can only receive one card on each ace, thus you cannot double down after splitting aces. If the dealer-in-the-machine has a blackjack, you only lose your initial bet. (No value as it is part of the 100% model.)

Resplitting of Aces

Good for the players. After you split your initial pair of aces, if you should receive another ace on one of your split aces, you can resplit that pair. Value: +0.03 percent.

No Splitting of Aces

Bad for the players. Value: -0.16 percent.

Splitting Pairs

Favorable rule for the player, most especially if you can double down after splitting. (No value as it is part of the 100% model.)

No Resplitting of Pairs

Bad for the players. Value: -0.02 percent.

No Splitting of Pairs

Bad for the players. Value: -0.21 percent.

Doubling After Splitting Pairs

Good rule for the player. (No value as it is part of the 100% model.)

Doubling on Three or More Cards

Favorable rule for the player. Value: +0.24 percent.

Insurance

If the dealer-in-the-machine has an ace as his up card you can insure your hand for up to half its value. Bad rule for basic strategy players. Never insure anything, even your own blackjack. However, insurance is a wonderful rule for card counters who will know exactly when to take it. Quite often the difference between a winning or losing session for a card counter is proper use of the insurance option. Even in video-blackjack games of one round before a shuffle, there will be times a card counter benefits from taking insurance. Value: -5.88 percent.

Early Surrender

The player has the option of surrendering his hand when he sees his first two cards. In exchange, he gets back half his bet—even if the dealer-in-the-machine has a blackjack. Very good option for basic strategy player. Great option for card counters. Value:+0.62 percent.

Late Surrender

Same as above except...and this is a BIG except...if the dealer has a blackjack, you lose your entire bet. Good option for player. Value: +0.03 percent.

Six-Card Winner

Favorable to the player. It is only slightly more favorable to card counters. You win if you get 21 or less with six cards. Value: +0.10 percent.

Five-Card Charlie

If you receive 21 with five cards, you win a bonus from the casino—usually two to one. This favors the player. Value: +.20 percent.

Seven-Seven-Seven 21

Dealer-in-the-machine will pay three to two if you can get three sevens. Value: +0.01 percent.

Six-Seven-Eight Suited

Favorable to the players if you don't change your basic strategy in an attempt to suit up, except in the case of a six-seven suited against the dealer-in-the machine's two. Value: +0.01 percent.

Over-Under 13

You make a side bet that the next hand dealt you will be either over 13 or under 13 on the first two cards. Aces count as one for this and the dealer takes all hands of 13. Very unfavorable rule for basic strategy players. Marginally helpful rule for certain card counters. Value: -6.56 percent for the over and -10.06 percent for the under.

Dealer Hits A,6 (Soft 17)

Bad rule for all players. Helps the dealer-in-the-machine improve an otherwise bad hand for the house. Value: -0.19 percent.

Red or Black

This is a bet where the player guesses what the color of the dealer-in-the-machine's face-up card will be. At first this would seem like an even game off the top but the house stipulates that if the two of the color you chose shows up, your bet is a push. This gives the house an advantage over the basic strategy player. Value: -3.85 percent.

Penetration

How many cards a dealer-in-the-machine deals is called penetration. If a game deals all the cards out, that's 100 percent penetration. For the basic strategy player, the depth of penetration is of little significance. However, for the card counter the depth of penetration is another key variable in determining whether to play a given game. The more penetration, the better the game. Video-blackjack games with Las Vegas Strip rules and 60 percent or more penetration are highly beatable games for the card counter.

Dealer Wins Pushes

All ties go to the dealer. The most devastating rule against the players. Value: -9.0 percent.

Blackjack Pays 1 to 1 (2 for 1)

Bad rule for the players. Value: -2.43 percent.

Blackjack Pays 2 to 1 (3 for 1)

Great rule for the players but you'll be hard pressed to find it on any of today's machines. Value: +2.32 percent.

Basic Strategy for Video Blackjack

Knowing how the game of video blackjack is played is not the same as knowing how to play the game. For every set of rules, there are distinct basic strategies designed to optimize one's chances of winning. This does not mean that you have to memorize dozens of basic strategies since the overwhelming majority of decisions that you will have to make are the same in all strategies. However, basic strategy has two major categories—single deck and multiple deck—and if you intend to play video blackjack, you must decide which strategy to memorize. Those of you who decide to play single and multiple deck games should seriously consider first mastering one and then mastering the other.

The best way to decide which one to memorize (or which to memorize first) is to check out the machines that you intend to play. Most video-blackjack machines deal from a single deck and thus it is probably preferable to memorize the single-deck strategies. However, some of the newer models use double decks (some even four decks). Would it hurt a player to use a single-deck strategy against a multiple-deck game or vice versa? Only marginally, since the strategies usually differ most on hands that don't occur with great regularity. But if you want to be the best player that you can be, you should know both strategies. In the war against the casinos, it's best to be fully armed. And remember: you can feel free to bring this book into the casino with you. If the video-blackjack games you've decided to play don't have a time limit on decision making, then you don't have to memorize any strategies. Just refer to this book and take your time. However, on positive-expectation machines, faster play gets in more hands and your edge can be realized more quickly with the more hands that you play. But remember that speed is only good if you don't make any mistakes. This rule holds true for video blackjack just as it does for video poker.

At first it might seem a daunting task, memorizing the several pages of material that are coming up, but don't let that stop you. In fact, if you spread your learning out over several weeks, doing a little at a time, you will readily assimilate the basic strategy you've selected.

A friendly caution is hereby given: don't play video black-jack without learning a basic strategy because players who trust their own instincts and ideas are giving the casino a monumental edge. You are better off skipping the game of video blackjack altogether and playing one of the other, less complex casino games than playing improperly at video blackjack. The casinos make a fortune from poor blackjack players of the table variety and video-blackjack variety. Do not join their regiment.

Since there are more single-deck video-blackjack games than multiple-deck ones, I have decided to give the single-deck basic strategy first. The left-hand column will contain the player's hand; the right-hand column will contain the decision you should make based on the dealer-in-the-machine's up card. How many cards compose a given hand is essentially irrele-vant except for splitting or doubling down purposes. For exam-ple, if you have a nine composed of two cards—a four and a five, or a three and a six, etc.—you would double down against any dealer-in-the-machine's up card of three through six. If you had a nine composed of three cards—say, a four, two and three—you would hit until you had 12 or more and then follow the basic strategy for that hand. Thus, if the dealer-in-the-machine is showing a six and you have a three-card nine, you would hit it. If you received a three, you would now have 12. The basic strategy calls for standing with a 12 against a dealer-in-the-machine's up card of six. Any hand which is 11 or under, no matter how many cards compose it, hit until you reach 12 or more and then follow the basic strategy for that hand. You never hit hard hands of 17 or more against anything.

If you have played blackjack before, but you haven't employed a basic strategy, some of these moves will seem strange. For example, many players blanch at hitting a hand of 12 against the dealer's two or three. Many players cringe when having to split a hand of 8,8 against a dealer's 10. Many of these moves do seem almost suicidal but in fact they are the proper strategies. Remember that millions of hands have been generated by computer to establish these basic strategy rules. And many of these rules are designed *to lose you less* in bad situations. Having 8,8 against a dealer's 10 is a losing hand. By splitting them, you decrease the total amount of your losses in this situation than if you hit or stood. So follow these basic strategies perfectly and don't allow any fools at the table to intimidate you into not hitting that 12 against a dealer's 2, or splitting those 8,8's against a dealer's 10. Also, keep in mind that all soft hands become hard hands when the ace can no longer be used as an 11.

Basic Strategy for Single-Deck Games

The single-deck game is the best game for the video-blackjack player to play, if the rules are liberal when it comes to doubling down and splitting. If you have the option of playing single-deck or multiple-deck games, you would be foolish to choose the latter. A single deck offers so many more opportunities for the basic-strategy player and the card counter alike.

Player's Hard Hand:	Decision based on dealer's up card:
8	Double against a 5 and 6. Hit against all else.
9	Double against 2 through 6. Hit against all else.
10	Double against 2 through 9. Hit against all else.
11	Double against everything.
12	Hit against 2 and 3. Stand against 4,5,6. Hit against all else.
13	Stand against 2 through 6. Hit against all else.
14	Stand against 2 through 6. Hit against all else.
15	Stand against 2 through 6. Hit against all else.

16 . . . . Stand against 2 through 6.
                                         Hit against all else.
(If surrender is allowed, surrender a 15 or 16 against a
dealer's 10.)
17, 18, 19, 20, 21 . . . . Stand against everything.

Player's Soft Hands:	**Decision based on dealer's up card:**
A,2	Double against 4, 5, 6. Hit against all else.
A,3	Double against 4, 5, 6. Hit against all else.
A,4	Double against 4, 5, 6. Hit against all else.
A,5	Double against 4, 5, 6. Hit against all else.
A,6	Double against 2 through 6. Hit against all else.
A,7	Double against 3,4,5,6. Stand on 2,7,8, ace. Hit against 9 and 10.
A,8	Double against a 6. Stand against all else.
A,9	Stand against everything.

Player's Pair:	**Decision based on dealer's up card:**
A,A	Split against everything.
2,2	Split against 3 through 7. Hit against all else.
3,3	Split against 4, 5, 6, 7. Hit against all else.
4,4	Double against 5 and 6. Hit against all else.
5,5	Double against 2 through 9. Hit against all else.
6,6	Split against 2 through 6. Hit against all else.

7,7 . . . . Split against a 2 through 7. Hit
                                        against 8, 9, ace. Stand against
                                        a 10.
(If surrender is allowed, surrender 7,7 against a dealer's 10.)
8,8 . . . . Split against everything.
(If surrender is allowed, surrender 8,8 against a dealer's 10.)
9,9 . . . . Split against 2 through 6; 8, 9.
                                        Stand against 7, 10, ace.
10,10 . . . . Stand against everything.

Additional Single-Deck Strategies

The single-deck video-blackjack game is quite different from the multiple-deck video-blackjack game because the composition of a given hand is actually an important factor in your decisions. For example, in a multiple deck any player's hand of 12 is to be treated as a equal to any other hand of 12. Not so with a single deck. A 10,2 is to be handled differently than, say, a 5,7 when facing a dealer's up card of 4. In the former situation, you would hit; in the latter situation, you would stand. Now, on the basic strategy for single deck, I have not added any of the refinements that follow because they will not drastically alter your long-run expectations. However, if you want to get an extra edge, I recommend you incorporate the following variations of play into your single-deck strategy.

1. Hit 10,2 against a dealer's 4. Stand on all other hard 12s.
2. Hit 10,3 and 9,4 against a dealer's 2. Stand on all other hard 13s.
3. Stand on any three or four card total of 16 against a dealer's 10.
4. Stand on a 9,7 against a dealer's 10. If surrender is allowed, however, you would surrender this hand as you would any 16 against a dealer's 10.
5. If you can double after splitting pairs:
   a.) split 2,2 against a dealer's 2.
   b.) split 3,3 against a dealer's 2 or 3.
   c.) split 4,4 against a dealer's 5 or 6.

Basic Strategy for Multiple-Deck Games

Player's Hard Hand:	Decision based on dealer's up card:
8	Hit against everything
9	Double against 3 through 6. Hit against everything else.
10	Double on 2 through 9. Hit on 10 and ace.
11	Double on 2 through 10. Hit on ace.
12	Hit against 2 and 3. Stand against 4, 5, 6. Hit against 7 through ace.
13	Stand against 2 through 6. Hit against all else.
14	Stand against 2 through 6. Hit against all else.
15	Stand against 2 through 6. Hit against all else.
16	Stand against 2 through 6. Hit against all else.

(If surrender is allowed, you will surrender a hand of 15 or 16 against a dealer's 10. You will surrender a 16 against a dealer's 9, 10 or ace.)

17,18,19,20, 21	Stand against everything.

Player's Soft Hand:	Decision based on dealer's up card:
A2	Double against 5 and 6. Hit against all else.
A3	Double against 5 and 6. Hit against all else.
A4	Double against 4,5,6. Hit against all else.
A5	Double against 4,5,6. Hit against all else.

A6 . . . . Double against 3,4,5,6.
                                                Hit against all else.
A7 . . . . Double against 3,4,5,6. Stand
                                                on 2,7,8, ace. Hit against 9
                                                and 10.
A8, A9 . . . . Stand against everything.

| | **Decision based on** |
| **Player's Pair:** | **dealer's up card:** |

A,A. . . . . Split against everything.
2,2. . . . . Split against 2 through 7.
                                                Hit against all else.
3,3 . . . . Split against 2 through 7.
                                                Hit against all else.
4,4 . . . . Split against 5 and 6. Hit
                                                against all else.
5,5 . . . . Double 2 through 9.
                                                Hit against all else.
6,6 . . . . Split against 2 through 6.
                                                Hit against all else.
7,7 . . . . Split against 2 through 7.
                                                Hit against all else.
8,8 . . . . Split against everything.
(If surrender is allowed, surrender 8,8 against a dealer's 10.)
9,9 . . . . Split 2 through 6; 8 and 9.
                                                Stand against 7,10, and ace.
10,10 . . . . Stand against everything.

If you are playing multiple-deck games, some machines
will allow you to double down after splitting pairs (some single-deck machine will allow this also). For example, if you have
2,2 and the dealer-in-the-machine is showing a five, you would
split your twos. Now, the dealer-in-the-machine deals you a
nine on the first two. You have 11. You would double down
your 11 in this situation. The rule of thumb is to treat either
half of a split the way you would a regular hand and follow the
basic strategy tables as indicated. Some machines might allow
you to resplit pairs up to four times. Thus, if you received a
2,2 and split and received another two, you would resplit and

so forth. These options are favorable to the player and should be taken advantage of.

Card Counting at Video Blackjack

Card counting for video blackjack is not difficult to learn. In fact, I think learning the theory of card counting is much easier than memorizing basic strategy. By the end of this section, you will know how to count cards. And you will be able to do so much more easily than a regular blackjack player because you won't have the added distractions of the other players, the dealers and the paranoid pit crews to cope with. Even video-blackjack games that deal just one round are susceptible to card counting—especially machines that allow you to play multiple hands. Thus, learning how to count cards is an important skill if you want victory at video blackjack.

The theory of card counting is quite simple: big cards favor the players, small cards favor the dealer-in-the-machine. This is a fact backed up by tens of millions of computer runs over four decades of blackjack study. Thus, as the game is progressing, if the deck contains more big cards (10s and aces) because more little cards have been played, it will be to the player's advantage. Whereas if the deck contains more little cards (twos through sixes), it will favor the dealer-in-the-machine. Of course, having a deck favor you is not the same as a guaranteed win, nor is having an unfavorable deck a guaranteed loss. However, in the long run analysis of blackjack, the player will win more hands when the decks contain high cards than he will lose, and he will lose more hands when the decks contain low cards than he will win.

Card counting systems take advantage of this fact in four ways:

1. All card counting systems keep track of the relationship of small cards to big cards in the remaining deck.

2. When the cards remaining in the deck favor the player, the player will bet larger sums of money. When the cards remaining in the deck favor the casino, the player will bet

smaller amounts or the minimum amount allowed.

3. Certain changes to basic strategy are made based on the "count" that increase a player's advantage or decrease his disadvantage when playing certain hands.

4. The use of the insurance option now becomes viable at certain times, even in single-round games.

If you have decided to learn how to count cards, you have another big decision to make. What card counting system will you use? There are literally dozens of different counting systems on the market, some selling for upwards of $295. To make matters worse, most of the card counting systems are good! There are card counting systems that keep track of every card in the deck; there are systems that are four level systems—that is, cards are assigned a value of +1 to +4 (and -1 to -4); there are three- and two-level systems. Some are so difficult and so elaborate that only a genius could play them. Some are so simple that mere mortals (you and me) can play them.

You are lucky for, unlike me, you don't have to attempt to play a representative sampling of all these systems before deciding which to choose. I did. I've played three-level counts, two-level counts and one-level counts with side counts of aces and fives. They all work.

Unfortunately, for me, they all work about as well as the simplest and easiest to learn and use—a one-level count, called the Hi-Lo Count, that only follows certain cards. Recent research, and blackjack is a well-researched game, has shown that there isn't much difference in performance between a good one-level count and a good multi-level count. The only real difference is the level of difficulty in learning and executing the multi-level as opposed to the single-level counts. So why bother wasting time learning a more difficult count when its advantage over a simpler count is minuscule?

So the count we'll deal with will be the Hi-Lo.

Here are the card values in the Hi-Lo counting system.

2 = +1	7 = 0	10 = -1
3 = +1	8 = 0	ace = -1
4 = +1	9 = 0	
5 = +1		
6 = +1		

As you are playing, if more small cards are coming out of the deck, you have what is called a *positive count*. If more large cards are coming out of the deck, you have what is called a *negative count*. After a round of play, if the count is positive, the next round should theoretically favor the player because a greater proportion of the large cards remain in the deck to be played. If the count is negative after a round of play, the next round favors the casino because a greater proportion of the small cards remain to be played.

Why do the large cards favor the player and small cards favor the house?

1. Large cards make a blackjack more likely. Although the player and the dealer-in-the-machine have an *equal* chance of getting a blackjack, the player is paid off at three to two *in some cases*. In these cases, if a player gets one blackjack in one round of play and the dealer-in-the-machine gets one blackjack in another round of play, the player comes out ahead, assuming his bets were the same in both rounds. The converse is also true. With small cards remaining in the deck, a blackjack is less likely.

2. Although the dealer-in-the-machine will get slightly better hands in a positive count (as will the player), when the dealer-in-the-machine has a bust hand (12 to 16), he is more likely to actually bust. The dealer-in-the-machine must hit his bust hands, but the player doesn't have to. In a negative count, the dealer-in-the-machine will hit his bust hand and is more likely to make a good hand because small cards are more likely to come out.

I want to reinforce what I said earlier. The fact that something is *more likely* to happen doesn't *guarantee* it *will* happen every time. When you count cards, you will have very high positive counts where the dealer-in-the-machine will draw to his bust hands and still get small cards. You will have negative counts where blackjacks appear—one after another. Over time, over the long run (whatever that is), what is more likely to happen will happen more often than what is less likely to happen.

Now, that you know the values of the cards, you have to hit upon a workable method for counting them. You have to keep a *running count* of the cards as they come out of the deck.

To become proficient, you have to put the practice in. Card counting is, as you have just seen, easy to understand, hard to actually do at first. However, once you master card counting, you never forget how to do it. Like riding a bike, counting cards and playing basic strategy can become second nature.

What should also become second nature are the variations in basic strategy required based on the count. There are literally hundreds of variations for both single and multiple-deck games. However, much like the numerous card-counting systems, memorizing hundreds of strategy variations will not yield you much value for your time. You are better off simply memorizing the few strategy variations for certain hands that occur with some regularity and in count ranges that you are more often likely to have. Thus, the following variations should be incorporated into your arsenal.

Variations in Single-Deck Basic Strategy

All strategy variations in single-deck games are based on the running count.

Running Count	Variation in Strategy
-1 or less	hit 13 against the dealer's 2 or 3
+1 or more	stand on 12 against the dealer's 2 or 3
	stand on 10,2 against dealer's 2, 3, or 4
	insure all hands against a dealer's ace
	double on 10 against a dealer's ace
+2 or more	stand on all 16s against a dealer's 10
	double A,8 against a dealer's 5

These few variations in strategy will help you considerably in playing certain hands. Remember that at a +1 or more, you insure all your hands against the dealer's ace—even the hands 11 or 10 which you are doubling down. The correct use of the insurance option in a single-deck game is probably the key variation to employ. Even if it is only you and the dealer-in-the-machine at a single-round game, if you have two small cards and the dealer is showing an ace, you would insure because the count is +1! You have a slight advantage.

Variations in Multiple-Deck Basic Strategy

Counting into a multiple-deck game is slightly more complicated than counting into a single-deck game because you have to keep track of two different counts—the *running count* and the *true count*. The running count is the count you keep as the game is progressing. Thus, if the following cards appear: 4, 8, 6, ace, 10, 5, 3, 2, 7, 4—you have a running count of +4 (4 = +1; 8 = 0; 6 = +1; ace = - 1; 10 = - 1; 5 = +1; 3 = + 1; 2 = + 1; 7 = 0; 4 = + 1). However, to establish whether a count actually means you have an edge over the casino (or whether the casino has an edge over you), you must divide the number of decks remaining to be played into your running count—this is your *true count* because it gives you a true indication of what is actually happening.

Say you have a running count of + 8 with two decks remaining to be played in a four-deck game, your true count would be + 4. You divided the decks remaining to be played, two, into your running count +8, which gives you a true count of +4.

Now, exactly what does this mean in terms of an edge? As a general rule of thumb, any positive true count equals a half percentage point in favor of the player. Thus, a true count of + 4 equals two percent in favor of the player. However, the casino has approximately a half percent on the player in a multiple-deck game so the above situation would give the player a 1.5 percent edge over the casino.

For a true count to be significant in a multiple-deck game, it should give you an edge of at least one percent or more. In a single deck game, you do not need to be able to get a true count in order to know whether you or the casino has the edge. Any negative count favors the casino and any positive count favors the player. You can, if you want, get a true count for a single deck game as well. This can be done by dividing the fraction of the decks remaining to be played into the running count—thus, a running count of + 3 with a half deck remaining would be a true count of + 6 because 0.5 divided into three equals six. However, in a multiple-deck game, the true count is the basis of all decisions and must be ascertained at all times.

True Count	Variation in Strategy
-2 or less	bet minimum
-1 or less	hit 13 against the dealer's 2 or 3
+2 or more	stand on 12 against a dealer's 2 or 3 double down on 11 against an ace stand on 16 made with three or more cards against the dealer's 10
+3 or more	insure every hand against the dealer's ace double down on 10 against the dealer's ace double down on 9 against a dealer's 2

Betting at Video Blackjack

The key to winning money in traditional blackjack play is to bet more when the count favors you, bet less when it doesn't. You can do this on machines that deal more than one round. Bet the minimum number of coins on the first round and in all negative counts and the maximum number of coins in any positive count.

On single-round machines, you should bet whatever you are comfortable with and use your card counting skills and basic strategy variations to get a small edge.

Money Management at Video Blackjack

By now it has become the ultimate cliché but like most clichés it's worth repeating—*gambling is streaky*. Therefore, to avoid being wiped out during a cold streak, the astute gambler must have enough of a bankroll to weather the storms of negativity that ultimately come his way. In video blackjack, a total bankroll of 200 times your *maximum* bet should be enough to sustain you through even the worst negative fluctuations. Of course, if you are playing a negative-expectancy machine that even with card counting and proper strategy yields less than you put in—for example, one where the machine keeps all pushes and pays two *for* one at blackjack—no money management can help you overcome the odds. The negative storms will ultimately swallow you.

However, there is no reason to play such machines since there are many decent video-blackjack games around. Even on some of the otherwise negative machines, card counting can give the skillful player a slight edge—or at least an even game. Just as in video-poker, the rules and paybacks determine which machines are worthwhile bets. However, unlike video poker, where more advanced analysis is necessary to determine the percentage edge on a machine, the video-blackjack machines reveal their secrets even to the non-mathematician. Just use the information in this book concerning rule variations to determine just what games are worth playing. Add the proper points when the rule or option favors the player, subtract the proper points when it favors the casinos. In this way, you can determine the house edge on all but the most obscure video-blackjack machines. With proper play and casino comps, many machines are a worthwhile gamble—indeed, some are better than their table-game cousins!

9

Victory at Video Craps

"I doubt if many casino gamblers would disagree with the following statement: craps is the single most exciting table game in the casinos. Some writers have compared it to the gambling equivalent of hitting a home run in the World Series—when you're winning. It can be exhilarating and exhausting. When you are losing it can be the gambling equivalent of the myth of Sisyphus, whose torment for all eternity was to roll a large boulder up a mountain and then, just as he got it to the top, see it roll all the way back down, where he had to start all over again. In a word, craps can be the ultimate in frustration." So I wrote in the opening of my chapter on craps in my book *Guerrilla Gambling: How to Beat the Casinos at Their Own Games!*

The video versions of craps are no less frustrating though somewhat less compelling and certainly less exciting to play. Gone is the sense of communion with the other players, and the shared, almost tribal, camaraderie of the "right" bettors as they root for their numbers to appear while simultaneously praying that that dreaded seven won't make its devastating appearance.

Like its table-game cousin, video craps is a game with a cornucopia of betting opportunities, most of them carrying an extremely large house edge. Just take a look at the craps layout on the screen and you can see that video craps is a bettor's paradise or hell. The craps layout has scared many a would-be player. Fortunately, for the astute craps player, there are only a few bets that are worth making. Unfortunately, for the video-craps player, several of these bets have been eliminated from the video version of the game including: the odds bets on Pass Line and Come wagers and place bets paying off at the house odds.

Still video-craps has a supermarket of betting options and this might lead some aficionados of the video scene to shy away from it. Don't. Video craps only *looks* complicated because of that host of essentially irrelevant bets marked on the screen. These bets take up most of the screen's space and are the junk food of video gambling. The Captain, the world's greatest craps player (see my book *Beat the Craps Out of the Casinos: How to Play Craps and Win!*), calls these bets Crazy Crapper bets because essentially you have to be crazy to make them. That's how high the house edge is on them. Indeed, some of the Crazy Crapper bets make some low-paying slot machines look overly generous!

With the exception of the bets mentioned previously and the inclusion of a better Field bet, the video version of craps has the same payouts, playing procedure and odds as its table-game namesake. Thus, an analysis of video-craps parallels an analysis of the table game version. (If the machine isn't rigged.)

The Odds of Video Craps

The pay structure of video craps reflects the pay structure of regular craps in most cases. That is, you are betting in relation to the seven's probability to show or, in the case of one-roll bets, the odds of that particular number being thrown in 36 trials. Thus, most craps bets are not even money affairs but offer interesting yet rarely generous odds.

But aren't the odds always fixed and based on pure mathematics?

Yes and no.

Unfortunately, as many of you know, there is a difference between "true odds" and "casino odds." In that difference lies the casinos' profits.

The true odds of a bet are based upon the probability of that particular event happening. For example, the number four can be made in three different ways with two dice—3:1; 2:2; 1:3—and thus it will theoretically come up once every 12 times because there are 36 possible combinations on two six-sided dice—$6 \times 6 = 36$. So the true odds against a four coming up on the next roll are always 11 to one.

The true odds of the number seven coming up (and as you know the number seven is the single most significant number in the game) are five to one because the seven can be made six ways: 6:1; 5:2; 4:3; 3:4; 2:5; 6:1. Six goes into 36 six times and thus the odds are always 5 to one against a seven being the next number rolled.

You always get the true odds *against something* by figuring how many times an event won't occur as opposed to how many times the event will occur. (You get the odds *for something* the opposite way!) The seven won't be rolled 30 times in 36 rolls but it will be rolled six times. Thus, the odds against a seven are 30 to 6, or 5 to one! That's because six goes into six once and six goes into 30 five times.

Another thing to remember about probability and odds-making is this: we are only talking the *theoretical* likelihood of an event and not the *predictive* likelihood of an event. Theoretically, the seven will show six times for every 36 rolls but in *actuality* it might show ten times, or no times on the *next* 36 rolls. However, the longer the dice are rolled, as the total rolls approach the millions and billions, you will start to see numbers coming up with a frequency close to their probability. Probability theory is *indicative* and not *predictive* in the short run fluctuations of a game of chance.

Now, if the casinos were offering a *fair game*, theoretically at the end of an infinite number of rolls of the dice, neither the casino nor the player would be ahead. Everyone would be tied.

If I bet one dollar that the next roll of the dice will be a seven, and it isn't, I lose one dollar. Theoretically, however, I will lose five times and win once on this proposition. I will lose five dollars. But I won once and was paid according to the true odds—five to one! Thus, I won five dollars when I won. I lost one dollar five times and won five dollars one time. Tie game. Fair game.

But the casinos aren't interested in giving you a fair game because they have to make money, not break even. After all, how could they pay to keep their establishments going, not to mention keeping their stockholders happy. So by slightly shifting their paybacks to favor themselves, the casinos make a great deal of money, especially on craps. Thus, on the above example of the seven, in a casino if I bet that one dollar on the next roll and the seven appears, I'll only be paid *four dollars* for my win, instead of five. The casino is actually taking 20 percent of my win. The casino is a partner when you win a bet, but you are a sole proprietor when you lose. Thus, the *house odds* are what the casino will actually pay on a given bet.

Now, before going into the details of how the game is actually played, let me give you a chart of all the bets you *shouldn't* make. All these bets are Crazy Crapper bets where the house has altered the true odds dramatically. I'm giving them to you now, instead of after explaining the game to you, so that you can see them and then *forget about them*. For a fuller discussion of these bets and the fundamentals of craps, I refer you to my book: *Beat the Craps Out of the Casinos: How to Play Craps and Win!*

Crazy Crapper Bets

Crapper Bet	True Odds	Casino Odds	Casino Edge
Hard 4 or 10	8 to 1	7 to 1	11.111%
Hard 6 or 8	10 to 1	9 to 1	9.090%
11 or 3	17 to 1	15 to 1	11.111%
12 or 2	35 to 1	30 to 1	13.890%
Any 7	5 to 1	4 to 1	16.667%
Any Craps	8 to 1	7 to 1	11.111%
Big 6 or Big 8	6 to 5	1 to 1	9.090%
Field Bet	19 to 17	1 to 1 (2 to 1 on 2,12)	5.263%

You can see from the above list that many craps bets are crappy, to put it in plain gamblese. What's worse, some casinos, knowing the stupidity of the players, have increased their margin of thievery on some of the above bets by playing games with the English language. Thus, in Las Vegas many casinos will pay 30 *for* 1 on the one roll 12 or 2 bet instead of 30 *to* 1. What this means is the player receives 30 units back for his bet should he win but included in this 30 units is his original one unit bet! On the 30 to 1 proposition, you receive 31 units back—your 30 unit win plus your one unit bet. This simply makes the proposition have a greater percentage in favor of the house—a whopping 16.667 percent! Still more robber-baronly, some of the Mississippi riverboats pay off at 29 *for* one—a hideous 19.44 percent in favor of the plantation..ah, I mean, the house. You will find the same shenanigans existing on the video-craps machines.

Now, what does an edge of, say, 19.44 percent actually mean? Bluntly, for every $1,000 you bet on that proposition, you will lose $194.40 in the long run. Not a very attractive proposition is it? So watch for the "for" when you bet and remember that this "for" always includes the original bet in its payout.

However, many video-craps games give the players a break when it comes to the Field bet, which is a bet that the next roll will be one of the following numbers: 2,3,4,9,10,11,12. The usual payout is even money if any one of the numbers hit and two to one if the 2 or 12 is hit. This effectively gives the house an edge of 5.26 percent. In video-craps it is not unusual to see the 12 (or 2) being paid off at three to one. This cuts the house edge on the field to 2.56 percent. Considering the very high vigorish on the average slot machine and even most video-poker machines, this is not such a bad bet. If you were to play the Field exclusively you would be playing a machine that returned 97.44 percent of all money put in it. Not a bad machine. However, there is a much better way to play video craps than even this enhanced Field bet.

Side bets aside, in reality, craps is a simple game—as it must be to lure all the fish who play it. It is largely a mathematically-oriented game completely based on a given number's probability of appearance in 36 rolls and/or its relationship to the probability of the seven appearing. Unless there is something wrong with the machine, the video version of the game is based purely on probability theory based on a random number generator—in our case, the shooter-in-the-machine! The following chart gives the numbers that can be made from two dice, each numbered one through six; how many ways these numbers are made, and the combinations that compose them. Remember that there are six sides to each die and thus 36 possible combinations that can be made from two dice.

How the Numbers Are Made

Number	Ways to Make	Combinations
2	one	1:1
3	two	2:1, 1:2
4	three	3:1, 2:2, 1:3
5	four	4:1, 3:2, 2:3, 1:4
6	five	5:1, 4:2, 3:3, 2:4, 1:5
7	six	6:1, 5:2, 4:3, 3:4, 2:5, 1:6
8	five	6:2, 5:3, 4:4, 3:5, 2:6
9	four	6:3, 5:4, 4:5, 3:6
10	three	6:4, 5:5, 4:6
11	two	6:5, 5:6
12	one	6:6

The table game begins when the stickman pushes five dice to the new shooter for the *Come Out* roll. In the video version, you put in the number of coins that you want to bet. The machine automatically credits these coins to you and you can bet one, two or more (usually up to ten) on the bets you select. Just as in regular craps, the video-craps player can bet on more than one result.

In the video-craps game, you do not have to follow the procedure for the table-game which would be to place a bet on either the *Pass Line* or the *Don't Pass Line.* for the Come-Out roll. You can start the game with any bet just by pressing the ROLL THE DICE button. However, since the Pass Line or Don't Pass bets with a house edge of only 1.4 percent are two of the best bets in video craps (the others being the Come and Don't Come), either of these would be the bets to make initially. In machine language, any of the four bets mentioned would make the video-craps machine a 98.6 percent payback machine. Not bad at all!

If the first roll is a seven or 11, the Pass Line wins even money. Those on the Don't Pass Line lose their bets. However, if the shooter-in-the-machine rolls a two or three on the Come Out roll, the Don't Pass wins even money, and the Pass loses. Should the shooter-in-the-machine roll a 12, the Pass loses but the Don't Pass pushes (no decision).

The shooter-in-the-machine will keep rolling Come Out rolls until it rolls a four, five, six, eight, nine, or 10. (Remember that you must press the ROLL button for a decision to be rendered.) These are called *point* numbers. Let us say the shooter-in-the-machine rolls a six. That now becomes the *point* and the machine will indicate either by lighting up the point number or, more likely, by entering the point (in this case a six) in a box labeled POINT NUMBER. For Pass Line bettors, the shooter-in-the-machine must roll another six before it rolls a seven in order to win. For Don't Pass bettors, the shooter-in-the-machine must roll the seven before a six for them to win.

Although in the long term mathematics of craps, the Don't Pass bettor has a slight edge over the Pass bettor, in reality this edge is so slight that it is essentially irrelevant. However, what is not irrelevant is the disparity of opportunity on or after a Come Out roll.

On the Come Out roll, the Pass Line bettor is in the driver's seat. That's because he wins on a seven or 11, and loses on a two, three or 12. Now, there are six ways to make a seven and two ways to make an 11, which gives the Pass Line bettor eight chances in 36 rolls for a win. However, there are four ways he can lose because the combined totals of two, three, and 12 can be made in four different ways. Thus, overall, the Pass Line shooter has a two to one advantage on the Come Out roll.

On the other hand, the Don't Pass bettor is at his most vulnerable on the Come Out because he theoretically loses eight times for every 36 rolls, but only wins three times on the two and three (remember, the Don't Pass bettor pushes on the

12—that's the casino's edge for this type of bet). Thus, the Don't Pass bettor faces odds of 8 to 3 against him on the Come Out.

Once the shooter-in-the-machine establishes a point, however, the nature of the game shifts dramatically in favor of the Don't Pass bettor. That's because the seven now becomes the standard for success or failure. The Pass Bettor must buck the odds against him, while the Don't Pass bettor has the odds heavily in his favor.

The following chart shows the relationship of every point number to the seven. Since most bettors are *right bettors*, that is they bet with the shooter-in-the-machine and against the seven, the chart is structured *against* the Pass Bettor. For example, the point number of four is made three ways in relation to the seven's six ways. The seven will come up six times for every three times of the four. Thus, the odds are two to one against the four. However, the Don't Pass bettor has odds of two to one *in his favor!*

Number	Seven Made: Number Made	True Odds
4	six ways to three ways	two to one
5	six ways to four ways	three to two
6	six ways to five ways	six to five
8	six ways to five ways	six to five
9	six ways to four ways	three to two
10	six ways to three ways	two to one

However, in the table-game the Pass Line bettor can help his cause somewhat by placing what are called *Odds* behind his Pass Line bet. The odds bets are paid off at *true* odds. Thus, if the point is four, and the shooter makes his point, the odds bet is paid off at two to one. The original Pass Line bet is only paid off at even money. It is usually recommended that Pass Line bettors take the maximum odds allowed. Unfortunately, all the versions of video-craps that I've researched for this book did not have the odds bet as a feature of their programming, nor did they have any version of place betting that paid the usual house odds of 9 to 5 on the four or ten; 7 to 5 on the five or nine; and 7 to 6 on the six or eight. All place bets were either unavailable or paid off at even money. That effectively eliminates playing any version of the *Captain's Supersystem* or *Five-Count* Place Betting strategies at video craps.

There are two other types of bets of which you should be aware: *Come Bets*, and *Don't Come Bets* With the knowledge of the Pass and Don't Pass bets, these other two will form the framework for your playing of the machine. These bets function precisely as the Pass Line and Don't Pass bets, usually with one exception—they must be placed after the shooter-in-the-machine has already established the point.

Let us say that the shooter-in-the-machine has established his point. You now place a bet in the Come area of the layout. If the shooter-in-the-machine rolls a seven or 11, you are a winner. If the shooter-in-the-machine rolls a two, three, or 12, you are a loser. Now, if the roll was a seven, the machine will pay off your Come bet and return both your original bet and its payoff since the shooter-in-the-machine has *sevened out* before making the point. However, if an 11 appears, you take your winnings and you have the option of leaving your original Come bet on the layout, increasing it, or taking it off. If a two, three, or 12 is thrown, your Come bet is lost and, if you wish to have another Come working, you must press the button on the layout.

Now, if and when the shooter-in-the-machine rolls a point number (four, five, six, eight, nine, or 10), the machine will take your Come bet and "place" it on the number. You will not be given the option of placing odds on it. To win a Come bet, the shooter must roll that number again before he rolls a seven.

The Don't Come works in just the opposite fashion. When you place your bet in the Don't Come box, a two or three will win even money but a seven or 11 will lose for you. A 12 will be a push. However, should the shooter-in-the-machine roll a point number, your Don't Come bet is "placed" in the lay portion of the number's box and now a seven will win the bet for you. However, if the shooter-in-the-machine rolls that number before rolling a seven, you lose. Like the Don't Pass, you can lay odds on the Don't Come bets as well.

The mathematics of craps gives the casinos an edge of 1.414 percent on the Pass and Come bets, and 1.402 on the Don't Pass and Don't Come bets. These are the only bets you should make at video craps if you want a chance to achieve victory.

Money Management and Playing Strategies

Since video craps is so much like regular craps, I wanted to get the Captain's opinion as to any recommended playing strategies that he might have. After all, the Captain has created the most extraordinary ways of playing regular craps— so much so that the casinos are actively discouraging players from playing his methods. The Captain had seen some video-craps machines in the past but he had never taken the time to study them—once he discovered he couldn't play his *Super-system* on them. However, I asked him to look into video craps and to give me any help he could. Here's what he had to say:

The Captain: For a machine, the payout on video craps is ex-
    traordinary, around 98.6 percent—if you stick to the Pass,
    Don't Pass, Come, Don't Come. Unfortunately, I don't re-
    ally see a clear-cut way of attacking the machine with
    any of my table-game methods. To play video craps you
    have to bet immediately and you have to play every roll.
    At regulation craps doing this would be asking for losses
    in the long run. However, you could use a variation of
    the 5-Count, I guess. Bet a single coin, the lowest possible
    unit, until the machine establishes a point. Then four
    more rolls of any numbers, then on the next point num-
    ber [4,5,6,8,9,10] go with a Come bet of two units or four
    units or more. On the next roll do the same thing. On the
    one after that another bet. You'll have four numbers
    working, three with two units or more, and one with one
    unit, and maybe the machine will be in a fluctuation
    where the seven isn't appearing. Even if you could use
    the 5-Count perfectly on a machine, which you can't, so
    much of my thinking revolves around human shooters
    who at times get into a rhythm, a rhythm which might
    shift the odds by taking the game out of a random mode
    and into a deterministic or somewhat deterministic
    mode. But this variation of the 5-Count would be about
    the best way to approach video craps.

Frank: What about bankroll requirements?

The Captain: I would say a hundred units would give a player staying power. Of course, there aren't that many video-craps machines in a single casino so if things were going bad, you wouldn't have many options, such as switching machines. Some casinos only have one machine—if they have any. But a hundred units would give you enough to take a good shot.

Frank: Since the Field bet is such a much better bet on many video-craps machines with its three to one payoff of the 12, would you recommend this bet?

The Captain: Obviously, in the short run, you could see the Field numbers coming up at a pleasant rate. But what makes the bet a mathematically better bet than it's table-game counterpart is a single shift on the 12, paying that three to one instead of two to one—but the 12 is a 35 to one shot. So it's not as great a giveaway in the short run as it seems. That 12 might not show often in the short run—it might not show at all. The slight mathematical reduction of the house's odds on this bet isn't great enough to make the Field a worthwhile bet. So I'd stick with the bets discussed and use that variation of the 5-Count. I would recommend playing real craps but I realize that many people play the machines because the machines are more affordable. Even low-limit craps games are expensive. A hundred dollars on a quarter video-craps machine will go a lot farther than that same hundred dollars on a five dollar minimum table. So video craps is an excellent option for the low stakes player. For the traditional slot-machine player, it would be a fabulous game because of the liberal payback. Those Pass and Come bets are a lot better than most paybacks on the slots—especially outside of Las Vegas where slot machines tend to be much tighter.

If you are playing video craps in a casino that has a slot club make sure that the machine is either linked to the central computer system or that a slot host is informed of your play. Often the novelty machines such as video craps are not considered a part of the casino's normal comping protocol. However, you deserve to get credit for your play, just as any other slot player or video-poker player, and sometimes this means simply asking a slot host to drop by and observe you every so often. Played correctly and with a full range of comps, you could conceivably play even or almost even with the house.

10

Victory at Video Keno

There is a certain amount of hyperbole in gaming writing—or any writing for that matter. After all, book jackets celebrate the positive in an attempt to get readers to purchase the book. My books are no exception. Take *Guerrilla Gambling: How to Beat the Casinos at Their Own Games!* An *intellectually-delayed* person (that's the Politically Correct term for "stupid") might think that that title implied that ALL casino games can be beaten. It doesn't. Because they can't. In fact, the title is quite clear upon a closer examination. Part of beating the casinos at their own games is *not* to play those games that you can't win or that give the casino such an edge that no amount of intelligent play and comps can give you a reasonable chance for success. Still, readers understand that we writers play up the positive. Readers, by the mere fact of their reading, tend to be smarter birds than those turkeys the casinos are always plucking for their eternal delight. Even some of my chapter headings can be somewhat misleading—well, not necessarily *misleading* as overly *optimistic*.

This is one.

You aren't going to get victory at video keno but I wanted to keep the chapter headings consistent.

Video keno is just like regular keno with some notable exceptions. You are allowed to play up to ten numbers of the 80 possible numbers represented on the screen. However, you can't play a "way" ticket as you can in regular keno. Nor are the jackpots as big for the long-shot picks—except on the progressive machines which might pay up to $100,000. Still, video keno has an allure that sets it apart from regular keno because it is a relatively fast game. You pick your numbers and then press the START button. It is possible to play some six games in one minute as opposed to maybe six games in an hour in regular keno. Thus, the video keno player is getting much more action than is the regular keno player. For many video-keno players this speed adds to the excitement of the game. In addition, the machines come in all denominations from five cents to five dollars and there is no question that such a range of playing options is another reason for video keno's gain in popularity with a widespread segment of the machine-playing public.

Its burgeoning popularity is probably also due to the fact that it is interactive like video poker. The player gets to make choices. But unlike video-poker, the player doesn't have to memorize or refer to elaborate strategy tables to help him in his decision making. So it is interactive but in a limited and non-threatening way. It also offers fabulous payouts for little investment. For example, you can win up to $2,500 for a 25 cent investment on some machines. Although these paybacks are long in coming and represent a house edge of prodigious proportions, they are alluring for the player who wishes to make a killing.

The Mechanics and Odds of Play

Video keno is not difficult to play. It is the machine version of a lottery after all. Attached to each machine is an electronic pencil that allows you to "check" off the number or numbers you wish to play. Once you place your coin or coins in, you check off which number or numbers you wish to play and then press the START button. Should you notice before you start the game that you have inadvertently selected a number you don't wish to play, there is an ERASE button that you can press. Once you hit the start button the machine will select 20 numbers at random. If your number or numbers match one or several of the numbers selected you win varying amounts.

But the odds are long and the casino has a devastating edge in video keno—just as it does in regular keno.

Theoretically, on a one-spot ticket you have a one in four chance of hitting. Since there are 80 numbers, one fourth of the numbers will be selected—that is, 20. Thus, your number has a one in four chance of being selected or odds of three to one of appearing. So far so good. However, here's the bad news. Just as the casinos do in craps and other games, the payout for a three *to* one hit is three *for* one. If you recall our discussion of the word "for" in the video craps and blackjack sections, you realize that the machine pays you back your original coin in that three. Thus, you are really only getting a two to one payout for a three to one hit. If the game were fair (fair meaning an "even game") you should have received four *for* one which is three *to* one. Since the casino is keeping one coin on a one-spot ticket, it has an effective edge over the player of 25 percent! Not a good state of affairs. So while the payout structure of video keno looks alluring, it is the allure of the flame for the moth.

The following chart gives you the percentages you face at video keno and the type of payback you can expect for a perfect hit on any spot ticket. The assumption is that you are playing one coin. However, on a ten-spot ticket, you have to play maximum coin to get the progressive jackpot. And all payouts include your original bet.

Spot	Hits	Probability	Odds	Typical Payback
1	1	1 in 4	3 to 1	3 coins
2	2	1 in 17	16 to 1	14 coins
3	3	1 in 72	71 to 1	40 coins
4	4	1 in 326	325 to 1	100 coins

5	5	1 in 1,551	1,550 to 1	800 coins
6	6	1 in 7,753	7,752 to 1	1,500 coins
7	7	1 in 40,979	40,978 to 1	7,760 coins
8	8	1 in 230,115	230,114 to 1	8,000 coins
9	9	1 in 1,380,688	1,380,687 to 1	9,000 coins
10	10	1 in 8,911,711	8,911,710 to 1	10,000 coins*

* or progressive jackpot

In the preceding chart, I have not taken into account the fact that on a multiple-spot ticket you will get payouts for having some of the numbers that have hit. The following chart will show you typical payouts for multiple-spot play. Remember there are 80 spots, of which you can play a maximum of ten.

Total Spots Played	Number Hit	Typical Payout
1	1	3 coins
2	2	14 coins
2	1	none
3	3	40 coins
3	2	2 coins
3	1	none
4	4	100 coins
4	3	3 coins
4	2	2 coins
4	1	none
5	5	800 coins
5	4	14 coins
5	3	2 coins
5	2 or 1	none
6	6	1500 coins
6	5	92 coins
6	4	4 coins
6	3	2 coins
6	2 or 1	none

7	7	7760 coins
7	6	348 coins
7	5	15 coins
7	4	2 coins
7	3	1 coin
7	2 or 1	none
8	8	8000 coins
8	7	1500 coins
8	6	112 coins
8	5	12 coins
8	4	1 coin
8	3 or fewer	none
9	9	9000 coins
9	8	4700 coins
9	7	352 coins
9	6	47 coins
9	5	3 coins
9	4	1 coin
9	3 or fewer	none
10	10	10,000 coins*
10	9	4800 coins
10	8	1000 coins
10	7	140 coins
10	6	28 coins
10	5	3 coins
10	4 or fewer	none

* or progressive = to win you must play the maximum coin

There really are no preferred ways to attack video keno since the edge of the casino is so high. However, some players enjoy placing bets in configurations or sectors, moving these sectors or configurations around depending on where the numbers are hitting. For example, on a ten-spot bet that is in a box shape, you can move your box around the screen with each play depending on where the numbers seemed to bunch up last time. This will have no effect on your long term economic outlook but it's a fun way to play. If a gun were put to my head and I was told play video keno or die—then I would look to couple numbers. One thing you will notice when you look at regular keno boards or video-keno boards for that matter is the number of times numbers appear in a coupled sequence (37,38; 54, 55,etc.). Of course, in a truly random game and in the long run all the numbers will appear with their expected frequency—but in the short run those couplings are an interesting blip on the computer screen of probability. So I'd play a ten-spot ticket and pick five couples.

Now, go out there and win a million. Oops, sorry, I forgot that I don't have to use hyperbole to end a chapter...

11

Do the Casinos Cheat at Video Games?

This is the exact sequence that started me thinking along the lines for this chapter: jack of diamonds, three of hearts, four of spades, five of spades, six of clubs. I was playing the 9/6—4,700 coin Jacks or Better Draw poker machine at the Rio in Las Vegas. Naturally, I held the four cards to the straight and discarded the jack.

Bingo! Another jack popped up to replace the jack that I had discarded.

"That happens a lot, doesn't it," said the beautiful AP, my wife and playing partner, who was playing her own 9/6—4,700 coin machine right next to me. It was a statement of fact.

"Does it?" I asked.

"I think so," she said. "I've noticed it a lot."

"I'll look for it," I said.

The very next time I had a four to a straight, it happened again. This time it was a ubiquitous eight that made its appearance when I needed an ace or nine.

"It happened again," I said to AP.

"It's happened three times to me this morning," said AP.

"You think the Rio rigged the computer?" I asked.

"I doubt it," she said. "If this machine is rigged it would be the manufacturer."

"You think it's made this way?" I asked. "Every time four cards to a straight comes up, the replacement card is the same as the discard?"

"That would give the casino some advantage, wouldn't it?" she said. "But I doubt if it would be every time—otherwise people would notice."

"We noticed," I said.

The next several times either one of us received four to a straight the replacement card was not the same as the discard. Then it happened again.

"There are 47 cards remaining in the deck," I said. "Three of them are the same as the discard. That's three in 47. We're seeing it half the time wouldn't you say?"

"Well, we're certainly seeing it more than six percent of the time, which is what the real likelihood of it being." (6.38% to be exact.)

So for several weeks, we kept track of the phenomena. We played the same two machines every day for an hour or so in the morning. Gradually, the phenomenon began to proportionally decrease. The proportional number of times a discard was replaced with the same card on four to a straight flattened out. However, by the end of our little experiment, there was still a feeling that something was amiss with these particular machines.

"About 25% of the hands have been replaced with the same card," said AP, looking over our records.

"It's not really a very big sampling," I cautioned her. "If we played several thousand four-to-a-straight hands, we would get a much better idea of whether this was a normal fluctuation or if the machine's computer has been fixed in some way. As it is, we played a 110 of these hands—and in the beginning we were getting it a lot but it's trailed off. Who knows?"

"But think of it," she mused. "Any hand can be tampered with. We just noticed this particular one. What if there are others, so subtle that we didn't notice them?"

"We'd be throwing our money away," I said. "We think we're playing a break-even machine and in reality we're being taken to the cleaners."

"It would be a dirty business," she said.

When AP and I arrived back in New York from our month-long sojourn in Las Vegas, I had an interesting surprise awaiting me. The September 1994 issue of Arnold Snyder's masterful, quarterly newsletter *Blackjack Forum* was in the mail. On page 35, Don Paymar, an excellent video-poker columnist and author *[Video Poker Precision Play]*, writes about his own feelings, based on his own playing experiences, that something might be amiss on "at least some machines" in Nevada.

He recounts observations of "too often receiving a card of the same rank as the discard, primarily when drawing one card to two pair or to a four-card straight. For example, discarding the jack from 4-5-6-7-J (not necessarily in that order) on a common Draw Poker machine, we too often receive another jack." He admits that in a small number of trials, it would not be unusual to see this unusual event occur in three of 16 such hands—since anything can and does happen in the short run. But according to Paymar it's happening much more frequently than that.

He writes: "How about records of dozens of playing sessions, and during every session getting a card of the same rank between 25% and 55% of the time, with an overall average of 43% instead of the expected 6.4% (three in 47)?"

Whenever someone harps your fear aright, you figure there must be something in it. Well, Paymar had harped my fear all right. While neither my, nor Paymar's more extensive experiences playing Draw Poker machines were enough to scientifically "prove" that something was seriously wrong with these machines—whether deliberately or accidentally— it was enough to make me consider the "possibility" that this was so.

So I contacted my computer expert, Dr. James Schneider (see my book, *Break the One-Armed Bandits!*) to see if he could shed some light on the subject of possible casino and/or manufacturer chicanery in the world of video poker.

Frank: I'm interested in casino and/or manufacturers cheating at video-poker. How it could be done and whether it is done.

Dr. Schneider: It can be done in any number of ways but I don't know if it is done. I think in the United States there must be some laws about it.

Frank: In Nevada, Colorado, and New Jersey and maybe some other places, the individual states or casino control commissions have rules that any game that is represented by cards must deal from a 52-card deck and be random. The games with jokers would deal from 53-card decks.

Dr. Schneider: The shuffles have to be random?

Frank: Yes…I think.

Dr. Schneider: You haven't actually talked to anyone from these commissions?

Frank: No.

Dr. Schneider: Or looked at their regulations?

Frank: No. It's a good point. I've just assumed that all the commissions have laws against such things because other writers have written that they do. The commissions are the next stop I guess. But let's discuss the random shuffle idea.

Dr. Schneider: A random shuffle doesn't preclude the house from having an edge. The payouts for the various hands would dictate what the house edge would be.

Frank: The machines show their payouts per hand and it's possible to calculate just what the house edge is. There's no secrecy there.

Dr. Schneider: Cheating then would have to concern the actual randomness of the shuffle. That would be the first place to look. Perhaps the machine has been programmed to never allow a royal flush. Or, only allow the royal flush half or three quarters of the time. If I take the three-quarter example, when the cards are dealt out, any time a king of hearts comes up, the ace of hearts is behind it. Thus there can never be a hearts royal flush. Let us assume that machine deals out 10 cards, the first five of which are visible…

Frank: Parallel dealing.

Dr. Schneider: Parallel dealing. The other cards are behind these first five. So behind the king of hearts would be the ace of hearts—*at all times*. You would never know this because when you had three or four cards to a royal flush in hearts, you wouldn't discard the king of hearts so you wouldn't ever see the ace of hearts. Or, if a player made a mistake and did discard it, it would be a curiosity that the ace was behind it. What I've just described wouldn't even be a subtle programming technique. You could program a color in its place. Four to a royal in hearts are red, the discard goes and you receive a black card—you might even get a high straight. The programming could even specify that a normal flush appear. So, you program the machine this way. You have a sequence of 10, jack, queen, and king of hearts. The fifth card is the six of diamonds. Behind it is sitting the ace of hearts. When you discard the six, that ace will show and you have yourself a royal flush. Now, the machine senses the ace and simply substitutes a four of hearts. The player gets a flush but doesn't get the royal. The player would never suspect a thing. The player would be happy he received the flush, a little disappointed that he didn't get the royal and the casino has successfully cheated the player.

[Here I explained to Dr. Schneider my concern that machines I had played in Las Vegas might be substituting like cards for discards in four-to-a-straight hands.]

Dr. Schneider: Such a situation could be happening. However, I doubt that a programmer for one of these companies, even if he were told to cheat the customer, would do so in such an obvious and unsubtle way. After all, you picked this up quickly and anyone who played for a decent length of time would pick this up also. The four-to-a-straight hand occurs frequently enough that a like-card replacing a discard would certainly be noticeable—especially if it were 20 percent of the time or more as you indicated. If it is happening, there could be a problem with the random number generator's programming. It would be a programming flaw, not an attempt to cheat.

Frank: You mean, the shuffle isn't actually random?

Dr. Schneider: Remember that there isn't actually a shuffle, just random numbers generated from a random number program that simulates what a shuffle would be. If there is a flaw in the random-number program, you might get a shadow effect—thus, the straight sequence has the discard card shadowed with a like card. That shadow effect could be involved with all the cards in a sequence. Maybe behind each one is a like card. It wasn't done on purpose, it's just a design flaw.

Frank: What if it's a serial deal, and not a parallel deal, as many of the newer machines are supposed to be? The sixth card off the top of the deck is the first card given for the first discard, second card off the top of the deck is given for the second discard and so forth? Just like regular dealer would do in a real card game.

Dr. Schneider: Just as a slight-of-hand artist would do with a real deck, a programmer could do with the program. This could be even more sophisticated than anything found on a parallel program. The program could wait to see what the player discarded and then always give a bad card—any bad card in a seemingly arbitrary way. No one would know the difference. No seeming pattern. Just bad draws. Say you had two jacks but simultaneously four cards to a royal flush. Also say the player opted to keep the two jacks and not go for the royal—the dealer would not give him a third jack or any other pair. This could be devastating. The player would just know he was losing an awful lot. Even bad players could get hurt more than normal.

Frank: That's a problem right there. Losing a lot wouldn't affect many players since they are used to losing a lot—they expect it. This could be going on and except for a few sharp players, no one would even sense it. In video poker, you tend to lose more sessions than win to begin with—even for expert players. But experts can keep the losses to the minimum and come roaring back when the big hands and sessions make their appearance.

Dr. Schneider: You think the natural tendencies of gamblers would play into a scheming programmer or casino?

Frank: Yes. The big hands just don't show up, or show up much less than they should. Who would know?

Dr. Schneider: I just don't see the casinos doing this because they don't have to do it. They structure the games and order the type of programs they want. If a casino wants to offer a good video game, it can; if it wants to offer a bad video game, it can. Why cheat?

Frank: Because competition is fierce. Because they want all the players to play in their places and not the competition's places and that means they even want good players to play in their places. But to take the good player's money, the casinos have to finagle a little. That would be reason to cheat. The good players will only play the best machines and the good players know exactly what these machines are. They won't play an inferior-paying machine. So lure the good players in with supposedly full-pay machines and cheat them so your casino can compete with the other casinos. It's cut-throat competition. That's the motivation to cheat. The more casinos—the more cheating, not the less cheating. Offer seemingly great paying machines but rig them.

Dr. Schneider: That's a little out of my field—why a casino would cheat. I still don't buy that they do. It would be dangerous—especially in states where the casino industry is regulated. Think of the impact on the public if it were ever proven that the video games are rigged. It would have a devastating effect on legalized gambling.

Frank: Probably. Yet, people still gamble in illegal gambling parlors where the house is composed of known crooks. But I do think you are right. Public sentiment would be a factor in keeping the casinos honest.

Dr. Schneider: That's the motivation for not cheating or programming such things as we've been discussing.

Frank: I've always wondered this—how can one program randomness? Isn't that a contradiction in terms?

Dr. Schneider: Yes, seemingly. Randomness is an interesting study because there are subtle, usually short-lived, patterns in everything. Randomness and probability work hand in hand. You therefore program randomness by making sure that the probabilities over a sufficiently long period of time work themselves out according to theory or as close to theory as to give you a 99 percent confidence rating in the integrity of the program. By the way sometimes they don't. Then, you have a problem. If you give yourself a wide enough range in your programming, millions and millions, or billions of trials, more than likely you will hit an approximation of randomness. That is good enough to assure an honest game.

Frank: Could a programmer program patterns into randomness and not be aware of it? And then it shows up?

Dr. Schneider: Anything is possible. It's unlikely that using the standard randomness programs that such a thing would happen but a chip could be faulty.

Frank: So you think what AP and I observed and what others have reported might be an error and not deliberate tinkering?

Dr. Schneider: It might be an error in either one of two places. First, it could very well be a programming error. I still would find it hard to believe that a programmer would cheat in such a clumsy way or that the casino industry would risk such a thing. Therefore if that pattern which you observed is real, then I have to think it's a shadow effect, a faulty chip, or something of that nature. Not deliberate cheating. So that's the first place an error might be. However, the second place the error might be is with the observers. You might have noticed a short-term pattern that was ephemeral. Think of how many hands of video poker you played before you started to notice this particular pattern. You might have played hundreds or even thousands of such hands—four-to-a-straight—and never had the situation appear—or, it appeared within a few appearances of its expected frequency—six percent of the time or thereabouts. Also think of how often that machine was played by others when you weren't there. Did they experience the same thing? So it could be that your observations are at fault, not the programming. The casino or the manufacturer is not cheating you. You are getting the game as it appears to be. The casino's edge is whatever is posted and that's all there is to it. This pattern isn't a long-range pattern, it's just a blip that comes and goes. You happened to catch the blip and recognize a pattern. That's how randomness works. At any point, there seems to be something meaningful, organized, and deliberate happening—except it really isn't and it soon disappears to be replaced by other seeming patterns. The whole is patternless—except that it fits our expectations based on probability theory.

Frank: So the only pattern—if the machine is programmed properly—is based on long-range probability?

Dr. Schneider: That's it.

Frank: Assuming honesty.

Dr. Schneider: Assuming honesty.

I thought I had laid my qualms to rest about the possibility of casinos and/or manufacturers cheating at video poker, when I was reminded of a series of articles and letters in *Blackjack Forum* in 1992-93 concerning video blackjack. I quickly went through my back issues.

There was a highly revealing short piece by Joel H. Friedman titled "Beware of SEGA Robo-Dealers" in the December 1992 issue. After discussing the excellent rules and payouts for the SEGA Blackjack Super Magic Vision model, rules and payouts that give the player a better than five percent advantage—if the game were "honest"—Friedman writes: "So how can casinos make money with a game that has such favorable rules? The SEGA handout lists as a feature of their machine, 'Operator selected percentages from 84% to 99% in one percent increments.' It seems that the blackjack rules are fixed, but the house edge is adjustable.'

The SEGA machines did not meet the regulatory requirements of Nevada, since they represented themselves as card games, when in reality they were slot machines. The difference between the two is easy to delineate: randomly shuffled card games manipulate the *payout schedule* to give the casino and/or player an edge, whereas a slot machine manipulates the *results*. It's the difference between a dealer shuffling and dealing honestly or a card mechanic who can decide which cards will come up next in order to help the house or player win more. In video-poker parlance, the former is a *random shuffle*, the latter a *non-random shuffle*.

The conclusion of Friedman's article stresses that SEGA machines can be found in casinos all over the world—especially on cruise ships, in Asia and in Europe.

In that same issue, Allan Pell writes "that outside of Nevada and New Jersey [or any locality that strictly controls casino practices] no protection exists for the unsuspecting player. In effect, the manufacturers are cheating you—legally that is! Devices may lure players with great rules, but the software can defeat you with everything from peeking and dealing seconds, to programming that prevents you from getting a blackjack in your lifetime. This also applies to other video games—seven out more in craps, etc. The machines can be programmed to defeat you, regardless of the supposed odds of the game."

Okay, after finishing Friedman's and Pell's excellent and informative articles, one would think that the safest course for a video-poker, video-blackjack, video-anything aficionado would be to play in regulated casinos where you were sure of the game you were getting. Remember, you want a game where randomness dictates the fall of the cards, the roll of the dice or whatever; you want a game where the *payout schedule* can be analyzed to show just what the percentages are and that these percentages reflect what is actually happening vis a vis the game you are playing. Let me repeat—a slot machine does not have to tell you what percentages you face, it's programmed to pay back whatever the casino wants it to give back. According to Mr. Handle (see my book *Break the One-Armed Bandits!*) slots in his casinos are programmed from 83 to 99 percent and that is generally the range for most reputable casinos in the country.

However, the very next issue of *Blackjack Forum* (March 1993) had a truly disturbing letter from an anonymous individual in New Jersey discussing the video-blackjack machines in some casinos in Atlantic City—a regulated state. This individual writes: "Upon questioning casino personnel, and the New Jersey Casino Control Commission people, the following comments were made: the casino slot manager says these [video-blackjack] machines were registered as *slot machines* [italics mine] and meet all the NJCCC regulations pertaining to slot devices. The NJCCC person agreed, noting that the game is a 'randomly' dealt video-poker game with a set payout of anywhere from 83% to 99%, which meets the NJCCC requirements."

The letter writer continues: "A slot mechanic employee told us he sets the payouts on these video-BJ machines the same as any other slot machine...he assured us that the payouts were different for each machine...If it is a so-called 'slot device' with a set payout, this game borders on being illegal, or at least a misrepresentation."

This is disturbing news because, if true, it would mean that the payout schedule on these machines had nothing to do with the actual payback percentages. If several video-blackjack machines of the exact same type are paying different amounts—then the game is misleading—and, sadly, my fellow video-poker, video-blackjack writers have unknowingly misled themselves and others as to the nature of the games being offered in New Jersey (and other states) because no one has bothered to research the regulated states' actual rules governing video-poker, video-blackjack, video-anything machines.

Finally, to fuel my frustration and mounting ire, the September 1993 issue of *Blackjack Forum*, once again has Allan Pell writing on these slot machines in video-machine clothing. In an article entitled "Rip-Off Robo-Dealers II," Pell goes after the Japanese video-game manufacturers for employing "an electronic variable hold—which in essence are dip switches (toggles) that vary the programming" on their machines. "All sorts of little tricks can be programmed in without your knowledge, like never dealing you an ace when your first card is a ten, etc. Programming tricks can overcome any set of rules with a seemingly positive expectation."

Pell also states that not only is the Japanese company SEGA selling these machines in the Pacific rim casinos but that cruise ships are loaded with them. In addition Pell states that "manufacturers like Sigma, Irem, International Games Technology, and Bally's operate and sell devices outside the regulated jurisdictions," the implication is that even machines that appear to be standard Las Vegas-type machines may actually use variable programming. Pell concludes his piece: "Expect to see new forms of electronic gambling introduced, but be wary. The game may look the same as a unit on the floor in Vegas, but it only takes a different chip inside it to turn it into a bankroll vampire."

So my quandary continues and I must return to the initial question of this chapter: Do Casinos Cheat at Video Poker and Other Video Games? Fact: the variable programming machines are out there, according to Pell and Friedman, on cruise ships and in non-regulated jurisdictions and in foreign casinos. Fact: we know, based on Dr. James Schneider's remarks, how easy it would be to fix machines so that they wouldn't really be random-shuffle machines. Fact: casinos exist for one reason and one reason only—to take your money (albeit in as pleasant a way as possible). Fact: both AP and I, and others, most notably Dan Paymar, have noticed some strange "patterns" on some draw poker machines—in a regulated state. Fact: the anonymous New Jersey letter writer apparently discovered this type of slot-machine-in-video-machine-clothing in Atlantic City casinos—another supposedly regulated venue.

So what do all these facts add up to? A big CAUTION. As Dr. Schneider said, it's hard to believe the casinos would risk the bad publicity inherent in the public finding out that they are less than honorable in executing their games. Still, some casinos do bar card counters at blackjack, or harass people who play the Captain's *Supersystem* in craps, both certainly less-than-honorable practices. Maybe only certain types of bad publicity would bother them, then?

So I had to do my homework. My fellow gaming writers have assumed that because New Jersey is a regulated state, its regulations are the same as Nevada concerning video-poker machines. Had anyone really bothered to talk to the members of the New Jersey Casino Control Commission or ask to see a copy of the regulations? If the anonymous letter writer in *Blackjack Forum* was right—New Jersey did not have the same rules governing video-poker machines as did Nevada.

I called the New Jersey Casino Control Commission to see if I could ease my fears or fuel my fire. After all, the control commissions of the various gaming jurisdictions set the rules that the casinos must abide by. Supposedly these commission exist to protect us—the players. I spoke with Tony DiFlorio who told me that while the video-poker machines must conform to the same payback percentage range as any other slot machine, that is 83% to 99% return, "they are considered slot machines" and that there are no separate requirements for them as in Nevada. When I asked him if they must be based on a totally random shuffling of the cards, and that each hand must theoretically appear with it expected frequency, he stated that there were only two criteria for the machine. The first—that it fall within the payback scheme (83% to 99%) and the second, that "every sequence be in the programming."

"But that means," I said, " that if a natural royal flush is a 40,000 to one shot, the machine could be programmed to pay it once in every 300,000 hands or more?"

"Yes," he said. "The machine has to have the royal flush sequence in the programming just as a slot machine would have to have for example the triple 7's but the frequency is up to the programming."

Two days later I received a set of the regulations from John M. Kovac, Administrative Practice Officer for the New Jersey Casino Control Commission concerning slot machines in New Jersey. No distinctions were made between video-poker and other slots. The information that Mr. DiFlorio had given me checked out. Indeed, the letter writer to *Blackjack Forum* had been correct. Video-poker machines in Atlantic City are slot machines and the probabilities are not necessarily the same as they would be for similar machines in Nevada. Remember, Nevada is based strictly on the random shuffling of 52 (or 53) cards. The hands will appear in the long run within their expected frequency range. This does not have to be so for New Jersey Casinos. The game will be random, yes, but random the way a slot machine is random—that is, based on a program that dictates the probabilties and not based on the probabiltiies in a 52 (or 53) card deck.

Well, there it is. The payback schedule on the front of the video-poker machines in Atlantic City can not be considered as an unquestionably accurate gauge as to the playability of a particular Atlantic City machine. It is theoretically possible to have a machine that appears to have a positive expectation when, in reality, it would be returning the minimum 83% because the programming is variable. Because video-poker machines in Atlantic City are considered slot machines, the payout schedule should be viewed just the way a payout schedule is viewed on a regular slot machine—as informational material only, not as an indication of the percentages inherent in the game.

Next, I spoke to Rex Carlson, Laboratory Manager of the Nevada Gaming Control. He assured me that the video-poker machines in Nevada must conform to the random shuffle principle "of a 52 card deck" and that "the programming cannot have any secondary decisions in it. If the royal flush is about to be dealt the machine can't say, 'No royal on this hand.' The machine also can't say, 'I've given out too many paybacks today, I'd better cut back on winning hands.'"

Then I asked him if the payout schedule is the only way a casino can get the edge in Nevada machines. "Yes," he confirmed. "If a player understands how to read the chart, the player can determine exactly what he faces, unlike a regular slot machine where the percentages are unknown." Had he ever heard of variable programming for video-poker machines? "Yes, in other areas of the country and in foreign countries you might find these machines but they violate the law in Nevada. Video poker in Nevada is a game of skill and luck. That skill factor must be there for a machine to be a video-poker machine. They are not slot machines."

Now, many of you who play in Atlantic City will be faced with a dilemma—should you continue to play? My guess—and it's only a guess mind you—is that most of the machines in Atlantic City are exactly like the ones in Las Vegas— that is they use a random shuffle with no variable programming and no secondary decisions, and the payout schedule is the deciding factor in determining the casino's edge. Why do I think this? A quick perusal of the payback charts shows that Atlantic City machines are rarely full pay. Most are ranging from 92% to 96% if the payout schedule is accurate. The average payback for all Atlantic City slot devices is approximately 92%. These are bad bets for the player and great money makers for the casinos. The Atlantic City machines are manufactured and programmed by the same companies that service Nevada—would it really be necessary to include a variable program in the Atlantic City video-poker machines to reduce them a few more percentage points—even though such a practice would be allowed? Hopefully, no. The operant word here is—*hopefully*.

Thus, if you are playing an Atlantic City video-poker machine with a 93% payback based on its payout chart, there's a decent chance that it is indeed a 93% payback and that all the sequences are in the programming based on their actual probability. (Why you would be playing this machine after reading this book is beyond me!) However, what if you should find that rare Atlantic City machine that seems to be a full pay-back? Here would be the opportunity for the casino to use a machine that makes "second decisions" and changes the percentages. Dilemma time. The seemingly better-paying machines might just be the worst paying ones! And the machine would be legal—rigged against you, misleading you, yes, but legal nevertheless.

The bottom line? Here it is. For those of you who can play in Nevada, assuming the problem of like-card discard was just a "blip" or at worst a programming flaw in some machines as Dr. Schneider suggested, all the strategies in this book can be confidently applied because the game is what it appears to be—video poker based on a random shuffle with no variable programing or secondary decisions. The hands will come up with their expectaed probability in the long run.

Unfortunately, I can't recommend the Atlantic City video-poker games because I can't be confident that the strategies outlined in this book would be the most effective strategies to play on variable programming machines or secondary decision machines—especially for the supposedly better-paying machines. If, for example, the royal flush is a one in 1,000,000 chance instead if a one in 40,000 chance in Atlantic City—a Draw Poker Jacks-or-Better hand such as ten of spades, jack of spades, queen of spades, king of spades and a king of hearts would probably return more by keeping the two kings and discarding the other cards. You might have to play the Atlantic City game based on the "a bird in the hand is worth two in the bush" principle. Take your little wins when you get them and be happy. For Atlantic City, the best principles to use would be the ones discussed in detail in my book *Break the One-Armed Bandits!* Choose a video-poker machine as you would choose a slot machine. Use Mr. Handle's revelations concerning where the loose machines can be found in a casino, and couple this with the Julian and Darwinian Slot Selection principles. Use the money management techniques of a slot player because you could be playing a slot machine dressed in video-poker machine's clothing.

But what of other jurisdictions in America? With gambling fever spreading like wild fire throughout the country how can players know what they're playing? They can if they take the time to look over the regulations governing the machine games in the casinos where they wish to play. All regulatory states must explain the criteria of their machines. New Jersey isn't cheating the players (technically)—the rules clearly show what their machines have to be—slot machines returning 83 to 99 percent. The fact that the players and gaming authorities assumed the New Jersey rules were the same as Nevada is their fault.

Let us take a look at two other popular gaming venues—Illinois and Colorado. The criteria for machines in Colorado makes no reference to video poker or any machine game of skill as a separate and distinct kind of machine game. Thus, some or all supposed video-poker machines in Colorado could conceivably have secondary or variable programming—as long as the paybacks range from a low of 80 percent to a high of 100 percent.

Not so with Illinois, however. The Illinois gaming board has made it clear that video poker is a fundamentally different machine game than regular slots (just as Nevada has). Here's the Illinois' regulation that does so:

> "Section 3000:660—Minimum Standards for Electronic Gaming Devices
>
> a) Electronic Gaming Devices shall pay out a mathematically demonstrable percentage of all amounts Wagered, which must not be less that eighty percent (80.0%) nor more than one hundred percent (100.0%) unless otherwise approved by the Administrator. Electronic Gaming Devices *that may be affected by player skill* [italics mine] must meet this standard when using a method of play that will provide the greatest return to the player over a period of continuous play."

The above regulation describes a video poker device because it mentions "skill" as a determining factor. But the Illinois board goes even further lest there be any misunderstanding. In section "b," line "8" the regulations state: "After selection of the game outcome, the Electronic Gaming Device must not make a variable secondary decision which affects the results shown to the player..." Bingo! You're getting an honest video-poker game.

In fact, if casinos don't want us to be suspicious of their video-poker and their other video games which are supposedly based at least partially on "skill," then each casino should be encouraged to post the rules and percentages that are governing the play of that machine. If a New Jersey casino is actually offering a real video-poker game and not a rigged one, a nice big sign proclaiming that fact should be in evidence. In fact, each machine version of a video-poker game should give the exact probabilities inherent in that particular version for each and every possible hand. This way we'll know whether the royal flush will come up once in 40,000 or so hands as theoretically it should or once in a million as it might if it is really a slot machine in video-poker machine clothing. I would not go so far as to ask the casinos to actually give us a win percentage based on expert play because then they couldn't count on players playing poorer machines. However, video-poker players want to believe they are playing video poker and not slots. They don't want their games rigged. Perhaps the casinos in venues whose regulations don't preclude the possibility of "rigging" machines should take the initiative and let the public know just what it is the public is playing. Otherwise, you'll never truly know if you're playing video poker or just a slot machine in video-poker-machine clothing. Until that time comes, you're better off researching which states protect their video-poker players and which states throw them to the wolves!

So next time you play at your favorite casinos, make a point of stopping by the Control Commission's booth on the casino floor and asking to see their slot and video-poker regulations.

12

The Bride of Bulletman

Let's soar with the eagles in this chapter, shall we? I had a choice to make here and I'm making a choice that is a little uncharacteristic of me. You see, the typical chapter I had in mind for this section would detail the philosophy and strategies of players who, like myself, play cautiously and think of themselves as mundane exploiters of possible player edges. While the mathematics of video poker is clear—proper play on full-pay machines will yield long-term wins, there's nothing spectacular or elevating in that and nothing all that unusual in someone achieving wins playing the proper strategies on the right machines. It's a given.

However, Chapter Eleven may have been a somewhat depressing read, especially for Atlantic City video-poker players. The distinct possibility that you are playing slot machines in video-poker machines' clothing is no doubt an irksome, pehaps deflating, thought. But take heart. Despite this, some people do well in Atlantic City video-poker games. As you will see in this chapter, at least one player has intuitively grasped the nature of the machines in this venue and has selected her game and the locations of her machines inside the casino accordingly. If there is such a thing as a "gambling instinct," this lady possesses it. She is truly the most devastating player to hit Atlantic City in the past decade.

So meet Angela and her husband Phil…ah? *Smith!* Angela teaches elementary school on Long Island, New York. She's been doing so for some 20 years. Her husband is also a teacher, in a high school, but his gaming claim to fame concerns the fact that he was the renowned "Bulletman" of football handicapping lore. I know Bulletman because he is an aficionado of the Captain's craps systems and we have had many interesting conversations concerning the Captain and his ideas.

However, Angela is the focus here because Angela is unique among Atlantic City video-poker players. For example, in 12 recent trips to Atlantic City, she has won the progressive jackpots on joker-poker machines 13 times! In addition to this, for the past six years Angela has not had a single losing trip to the resort town by the ocean. That is remarkable. That is unheard of. That is why I want to profile her—despite the fact that she probably violates all the rules I've set down for proper play; despite the fact that she relies on "intuition" as much as on logic and computer studies.

What follows is a transcript of a free-flowing conversation I had with both Angela and Phil concerning her video-poker prowess and gambling in general. It is the story of a gambling couple from the very first time they went to Vegas until they became "regulars" in Atlantic City. I think it is instructive because I see Angela and Phil as the quintessential "recreational" gamblers. Their joy and their delight come as much from the playing of their games as in the beating of the casinos. They are, in fact, the everyman and everywoman of casinoland—except for one thing: Angela is a monster winner, and a prodigious, Herculean player as you will see.

How close is her playing style to the playing style I use? Night and day. That's because she literally plays night and day, putting in extraordinary time at the machines. She also eschews little wins and always looks for "the big score." Thus, she makes for an interesting contrast to my usual advice; advice that is based on my style of play—which is far more methodical and workmanlike. Indeed, Angela is not a player from my school of thought. Far from it. She has her own school. She is a firm believer in her intuition and she claims to have a certain "feel" for machines. If her phenomenal success the past six years is any indication, I'd say her "feel" is real.

As with so many people who are interviewed for gambling articles and books, both Angela and Phil did not want their real last names used. We had to find pseudonyms for them both. So let's open there:

Angela: I was thinking maybe a good name for me would be Mrs. Bulletman.

Phil: Mr. and Mrs. Bulletman.

Angela: Right.

Frank: I thought you [Phil] wouldn't want to use Bulletman?

Angela: You used Bulletman in the other book (*Break the One-Armed Bandits!*).

Frank: But that was Phil's humorous analysis of slot machines.

Angela: Well, I like being Mrs. Bulletman because our friends will know who I am and Phil's friends will know who he is but no one else will.

Frank: Okay. Mr. and Mrs. Bulletman you will be. I'll title the chapter…

Angela: You were originally going to call it "Angela, the monster." I don't think I like that.

Frank: How about the Bride of Bulletman? B-O-B?

Bulletman: The important thing here is that Angela [B-O-B] grew up in a family and an environment where gambling was frowned upon. In spite of the fact that her uncles were bookmakers.

B-O-B: My mother's side of the family was just not a gambling family…no vices really. It comes to me in the blood from my father's side where they were bookmakers and poker players and every family meeting was a poker game or card game of some sort. I knew how to play poker from when I was little. My mother's side was the theatre and trips to the city [New York City]. They were the Manhattanites. You know Bonwit Tellers and that sort of thing. So I got it from all my aunts and uncles and from my father's side. Growing up I lost my interest in gambling so that by the time I was a young adult, I had no interest whatsoever in gambling. So when he wanted to go to Las Vegas on our honeymoon, it was a fight.

Bulletman: Not exactly a fight. A negotiation. As you know, I was always a gambler. I grew up playing cards from junior high school for money. When I was in high school I was always playing. But I never got to go to a casino because there were no casinos to go to, except for Vegas and as I kid that was out of the question. But when it came time to go on our honeymoon I tried to negotiate this Vegas thing because neither one of us wanted to spend time on a beach. I mean we both lived on the beach right here on Long Island. We can walk to the beach. Why go away and sit on a beach? So it was Vegas. I knew she liked to see shows so I used that as a…

Frank: Wedge?

B-O-B: Negotiation point. He told me I was going to get this room with mirrors with a great view and all these things. So I agreed.

Bulletman: So we went to the old MGM [now BALLY's], prior to the fire, and we booked four days and we took travelers checks for fifty-dollar amounts and in each pocket in my sports coat we gave ourselves a session's amount.

B-O-B: When you think about it, it was your idea of money management before we ever knew you.

Bulletman: In those days you could bring a hundred dollars to a casino for a day. Imagine doing that today? So we go to Vegas and we walk through the casino and we are mesmerized. Remember that you have to go through the casino to get to anywhere else in the hotel.

B-O-B: The place was fantastic. Life-sized portraits of all the movie stars. So I knew to get to the room I had to make a right at Judy Garland and a left at Mickey Rooney. That the bathrooms were by Elizabeth Taylor. I was star struck to begin with. But once I hit that casino I never looked back. My mother had given me this beautiful winter-white suit to wear. Just beautiful.

Bulletman: We didn't even unpack. We said, "Let's see what it's like in the casino." There were one-dollar blackjack games, five-cent slots.

B-O-B: I didn't stay with him because he was going to play the table games and I wanted to play the slots. I was so nervous on the plane ride going to Vegas that Bulletman would lose all our money on the first day. I mean this is what I worried about on the whole plane ride going there. I was so nervous. So angry that we were going to Vegas. Then we hit the casino and we didn't meet again until dinner. We still hadn't unpacked.

Bulletman: We couldn't eat dinner fast enough. We ate dinner in about a half an hour. Then went right back into the casino.

B-O-B: We gambled until about six or six-thirty the next morning!

Bulletman: Then we decided that, hey, we're going to be here for a few days, we better get some rest. So we go back to the room to get some sleep.

B-O-B: We looked at my white jacket when we got back to the room and the entire arm was black! From handling coins and pulling the lever of the slot machine my hands and my arm were black! I ruined the jacket. Pulling the machine handle.

Bulletman: So we're laying in bed, knowing the casinos are open for 24 hours, and I'm thinking to myself—"Am I going to sleep?" So I say to her: "Are you going to sleep? I'm not going to sleep." So we go back down. For some reason or other I decide to have a screw driver. Actually, I wanted orange juice but I figured I was in a casino, what the heck, I might as well have vodka and orange juice. This is now 12:30 in the afternoon on our second day and we haven't even rested. I have a few of these screw drivers. By late afternoon, I had accumulated about $500 worth of chips, which was a lot of money because I was only playing five dollars a hand at blackjack. But I wasn't feeling too good so I told her that I had to go upstairs to rest. For the next 24 hours I have this stomach virus. The screwdrivers just aggravated whatever this was.

B-O-B: He gets this all the time.

Bulletman: At first she's saying how bad she feels for me, on my honeymoon and all.

B-O-B: I'm trying to be the good wife. I'm rubbing his back and I'm feeding him ice chips from the ice bucket. I'm doing everything to be the good wife. But in the back of my mind there's the thought that downstairs is the casino.

Bulletman: The next thing is I close my eyes and then I wake up. I don't know what time it is. I don't even know where I am. She's gone. I look at the bureau. The $500 in chips is gone. I think, "Oh, God, she's taken all the money." The ice is all melted in the bucket. And all I can see is that white jacket with the black arm. I'm thinking that she's lost all the money. Then I sleep again. When I wake up I don't know what time it is but she comes back into the room. She looks miserable. She says: "I'm so sorry, I'll never do it again." She had lost the entire $500. And I'm thinking that she's become a monster.

B-O-B: So we're in the room and I'm taking care of him. I'm saying, "What can I do for you, honey. Let me know if there's anything I can do." And I'm thinking I want to get down to the machines. Finally, I convinced him to let me take some of the travelers checks and try my luck again. Since he was sick he hadn't used any of his. That's how I rationalized it. I had lost all of mine but we had all of his left.

Bulletman: She comes back about midnight, stays in the room for about an hour and then goes down again. From then on I barely saw her.

B-O-B: One of the dealers, who had seen me playing every-day, asked me out on a date. I was insulted. I said: "Can't you see that I'm a married woman? I'm on my honey-moon." And he said: "Lady, I've seen you every day and I haven't seen you with a man yet!"

Bulletman: That was essentially our honeymoon. On the day we're leaving, I may have seen her about four hours the whole trip, I have to drag her away from the machines at the airport. The announcer is making the last call for our flight and she's still playing the machines. I had to liter-ally drag her to the plane.

B-O-B: He did almost drag me.

Bulletman: We left coins in the trays. We barely made the flight.

Frank: And that was the creation of the monster?

Bulletman: And that's when the monster was truly born.

Frank: Yet, instead of becoming one of the hordes of losers, B-O-B actually became a winning player, or at least, a player who has a great chance of winning. She on the road to legendhood. Why's that?

B-O-B: Well, it didn't happen overnight. And it wasn't smooth.

Bulletman: It was an evolution. The evolution of a video-poker maniac. A year later we want to spend our anniversary in Atlantic City. Atlantic City was just geting casino gambling.

B-O-B: This time we decide to stay for a weekend at Caesars in Atlantic City and we take $200. We get to the casino and the man says to Bulletman: "Sorry, sir, but you can't get into the casino without a jacket." We went into AC and we walked all over the place looking for a place to buy a jacket. We asked one of the hotel workers where I could get a jacket that was reasonable. The hotel men's shops had jackets but they were all $300. We only had $200. So we finally found a shop that was reasonable and we bought a jacket for $50. So now we're down $50. The blackjack turns out to be $25 minimums. Maybe one or two tables with $10 minimums but you can't get near them. So I go over to play the slot machines—I don't even know if there were video-poker machines at this time. If there were, they weren't a big thing. A few minutes later, I feel a tap on my shoulder. We hadn't even checked in and he says that we're going home. He had lost all the money. We hadn't even spent the night.

Bulletman: It was about midnight or one in the morning and we go out to valet and…

B-O-B: They had lost the keys to our car.

Bulletman: Some first trip to Atlantic City this was!

B-O-B: Then we had to stop every five or ten miles to get gas because at that time…

Bulletman: That was 1978 and the gas rationing.

B-O-B: So we didn't even know if we would make it back home.

Bulletman: I figured that this would cure her of any desire to gamble but it didn't.

B-O-B: What I realized was you needed a decent-sized bankroll to go to Atlantic City. You can't play with scared money. You can't have only a couple-of-hundred bucks if you wanted to play blackjack. Now, even with the video poker this is true. I have a very big bankroll because I know how streaky the game is. I can weather any storm.

Bulletman: So we saved up a bankroll. When we went back next, we went with some friends who were fully comped.

B-O-B: That was impressive. We were treated so well. You could name the time you wanted dinner. The reservaions were made for you. They ushered you in. "How good to see you Mr. an Mrs. so and so." Just great.

Frank: You were the masters of the universe.

Bulletman: Right.

B-O-B: That did it for me. That night I hit on a slot machine. I won $600. I split it with my girlfriend because we had put up the money together. After that I decided to see what it would take for us to get comped.

Bulletman: When we first went to Atlantic City, we weren't comped. We had to pay full room rates. I think at the time it was about $150 for a weekend night.

B-O-B: But as we started playing more and more, we started to be courted. Our weekend room rates fell to a $100, then $75, then $45, then fully comped.

Bulletman: When we really started getting comped was when the casinos began with their computer tracking of machine players. B-O-B always puts in long hours at the machines. But before that, I was always hesitant to ask for comps. I felt funny about asking for something. It was a psychological thing. You've written about that in your books—to always ask for everything you can get.

Frank: I write that to remind myself because I used to have that problem of feeling funny about asking for a comp. I have to overcome that.

B-O-B: I don't have that problem.

Frank: When did you discover video poker?

B-O-B: I think I played them the way you would play the slots. I wasn't really that conscious of them. But when I won my first jackpot, I realized that I enjoyed this game more than slots. It just seemed easier to win at them. It's skill and knowing that every so often something will happen. At the casino where we go, I know the exact machines to play. Which areas they're found in. I know the exact machines. I only play the progressives in Atlantic City. I know that video-poker machines are supposed to be based on their payout scale but in Atlantic City I'm willing to swear that some machines are loose and some are tight—even the exact same machines. Playing so much has shown me which machines these are.

Frank: How long do you play for.

B-O-B: I'll play for ten straight hours at one machine in a carousel. I know everyone in the place. I know which machines are loose. I always play machines that have hit a lot. I prefer to play these because they keep hitting.

Frank: I think you've discovered the secret of the Atlantic City machines. They are very much like slot machines and their placement probably follows the placement philosophy of Mr. Handle [see *Break the One-Armed Bandits!*]. So you know where to find the loose machines.

B-O-B: I am a joker poker player…

Bulletman: A joker-poker fanatic.

B-O-B: Exclusively. That's my game. And I only play the progressives. Now in joker poker, you want to get five of a kind. But to get this, you have to be willing to spend a long time playing. You need a big bankroll.

Frank: So you combine bankroll with machine selection and you stick to joker poker only?

B-O-B: That's right.

Frank: You play ten hours straight—how do you do that?

B-O-B: Right from breakfast to the machines and except for bathroom breaks when I have them hold my machine for me, I just play and play and play until it's time for dinner. After dinner I'll hit the machines again.

Bulletman: She combines a solid strategy with enough of a bankroll. She also plays fast. She is like lightning.

B-O-B: I also must say that I do have hunches.

Bulletman: The amount she's won, some of our friends jokingly say that she was born with a horseshoe, uh, around her neck.

B-O-B: Well, they don't say *around my neck*. It's a slightly more colorful expression.

Frank: I get the idea. Somewhat scatological. The point is…you're lucky.

B-O-B: Yes.

Bulletman: How do you factor in luck?

Frank: I wish I knew.

B-O-B: I do have hunches about progressives. At a certain point, rows are about to pop. Some machine in the row will go. It might be because the progressive is at a certain level or whatever. But I can tell when a progressive is about to go. I can't always pick the machine that will win it but I'm usually there when the progressive is won.

Frank: Well you've been there and you've won much more than anyone I've ever heard about in such a short period of time. I've heard of people winning two, sometimes three times but never what you've done.

B-O-B: I see the game through. I'll play at a carousel that I know will hit. I'll put in the time. And I always feel that I have a chance for the big one. I'm confident.

Bulletman: Part of her success is a positive attitude. She's upbeat and confident. Even though much of casino gambling is supposedly cut-and-dry, I think what makes her such a winner is this positive attitude.

B-O-B: It's a personality type. I'm not a sore gambler. Win or lose, I have a good time. I don't complain. I'm happy to be in the game. Win or lose. You can't be negative. There's always that luck factor and you waste your time cursing your luck if you are losing. Why play if playing makes you miserable? I'm not afraid of losing and I don't fear losing. I'm going to go bang it out. When I say good-bye to Bulletman, I say to him: "I'm going to go bang it out." And I mean it. I go into the game with a determination that I'm going to win. You actually have to have physical stamina to play the way I do. I'd give up all the comp if I could have someone behind me massaging me. That's so much better than the drinks lady who comes by.

I'm probably the only person who loses weight when I go to a casino. I don't eat much, I don't drink much. I'm like a fighter. I have to be in form. A good massage therapist rubbing my shoulders when I play would be heaven. So I don't go in there worrying about losing my money. I go in expecting to win. I'm going to bang it out.

Frank: What about the actual playing of the hands?

B-O-B: I'm a big player. I go for the big win.

Bulletman: She has a look. We call it the original look. It's the look she had when she won her first jackpot. I could be playing craps [Bulletman's game is craps] and I'll see her coming from across the casino and she'll have that look. She'll be holding in her hand a ticket that tells you how much you've won. I know that look. She'll start giggling. One day she won two progressive jackpots a couple of hours apart. She came up to me and she looked happy but different. Then she showed me how much she had just won. It was flabbergasting.

B-O-B: I tend to discard weaker hands, even payable ones. A lot of people play for the little wins. I go for the bigger ones. I'll discard four cards and just keep a joker because I'm going for five of a kind.

Frank: Why video poker and not the table games?

B-O-B: Because there's no rivalry at the machines. We're like one family. I'll sometimes give advice on how to play a certain hand. People give me advice. It's all very friendly. I don't find that at the tables. If I were going to play table games, I'd play craps. But at the machines I notice that people don't take the game as seriously as do the table-game players. There the players can be downright nasty when they're losing. When you win at the machines, even if some people might get jealous, they congratulate you. We exchange tales of what happened last trip, or yesterday. But getting back to strategy. Most people play conservatively. I tend not to go for straights. I'd rather discard that potential straight and go for a better hand. That might be one of the reasons I've won so many jackpots. Throwing away an entire hand, I've been dealt straight flushes, four of a kind, five of a kind. So I'm not afraid to take that chance. I'll rarely throw away a pair. The only time I throw a pair away is usually for the straight flush.

Frank: When you have won a jackpot, do you quit?

B-O-B: Yes. I relax a little.

Frank: Do you quit for the trip or just for a short period of time?

B-O-B: I quit to take a breath... Not very long. I never would have won two progressive jackpots in a row if I had quit for the day.

Bulletman: The next day, she hit another jackpot.

Frank: That was three jackpots in two days?

Bulletman: Here.

[At this point bulletman hands me a photostat with all of B-O-B's winning jackpot tickets and there are the three jackpots in two days. Incredible.]

B-O-B: I thought I was invincible after that trip. The only thing we had to worry about was the taxes. We went back a few weeks later and sure enough I hit again.

Frank: You talk about a feel for a machine? What do you mean?

B-O-B: Machines run in cycles. That's my experience. In a ten-minute period a machine will hit a string of relatively large winners. Then, all of a sudden, nothing happens.

You could conceivably lose a thousand coins in an hour. Machines very rarely are choppy. They are either blazing or cold. That's been my experience. You're either doing very well or you're putting much too much money in. There doesn't seem to be an in between.

Bulletman: What gambling isn't streaky?

B-O-B: But this is so pronounced.

Frank: Do you ever have a "feel" that when things are cold they're going to get hot again? If so, what do you do?

B-O-B: Yes. In a case like that I'll stay with a machine because I just know it's a good machine getting ready to hit. You have to ride out the bad times. That's why bankroll is such an important factor.

Frank: You realize that some of what you're saying defies the traditional ways of looking at machines. Most gambling writers would dismiss the idea of "intuition." Even if such a thing existed, it would not be transferable. How can you teach someone to be intuitive? So intuition is generally put down as a superstition. What do you think?

B-O-B: Well, it may be superstition but I do trust my instincts. And so far so good.

Frank: Do you leave machines that are cold where you don't "feel" as if anything is going to happen?

B-O-B: Oh, yes. The worst thing that ever happened to me was some guy who was sitting next to me and he was drunk. Picture this now. He was hitting the buttons with his tongue! It was disgusting. Now, the machine I was on was a good machine, one I had won on quite often in the past. I was even winning this night. But I just couldn't stand sitting next to this drunk. He smelled. His tongue was coated. I mean, I felt as if I was going to throw up. So

I decided to move. I moved across the aisle to another machine, just to be away from him. The guy puts some coins into my former machine, hits it with his disgusting tongue and wins the jackpot! Now, I know from reading your other book [*Break the One-Armed Bandits!*] that I probably wouldn't have won a jackpot at that moment because the machine is constantly making decisions but it was just typical of a bad streak.

Frank: You were in a kind of tongue depression?

B-O-B: That was awful. Your pun. The guy was awful too. My attitude now is that I don't worry about someone winning big near me because I know that sooner or later I'll win on another machine.

Frank: Maybe I've asked this before , but why do you play?

B-O-B: I love to play. I'm in a zone. It's my total escape from all the world. But it is a social thing too. I'm a bit of a yenta [someone who likes to talk and socialize] and I get to know all the people around me. It's the same people who go to the same area—because we've all had a good experience on these machines.

Frank: Explain the zone idea.

B-O-B: I'm communing with the machine. This is very strange. You want me to talk about this?

Frank: It's exactly what I want. Commune with those machines. My book is rather dry, pages and pages of strategies. It could use a little more communing. So commune away.

B-O-B: It's as if I'm hypnotized. I'm in another world. It's just me and the machine. I feel as if it's a symbiosis between me and the machine. I just concentrate on the machine and in some way the machine is concentrating on me.

Bulletman: Robo-player!

B-O-B: Go ahead and laugh. But it's like I have a rapport with the machine. It's almost as if the machine is human to me. It's almost as if the machine has a kind of consciousness and it's a chess match between me and the machine. It's crazy. I sound crazy.

Frank: You aren't as crazy as you think. In *The Physics of Immortality* (Doubleday), Frank J. Tipler talks about the possibility of machines having a kind of consciousness. I'm not kidding. Not just computers but any kind of sophisticated machine. So maybe what you're experiencing is an advanced state of consciousness or an alternate state of consciousness. Of course, what you experience is probably what others experience too but they can't put it into words. You're able to put this feeling into words.

B-O-B: I'm communing with the machine and I'm lost in my own world. The troubles of the everyday world just vanish. I never get tired of playing. I never want to stop playing although sometimes I do take short breaks.

Bulletman: The reason B-O-B goes for the better hands is to give her enough money to sustain herself for long sessions. She's not afraid of losing but she is afraid of not having enough to last a trip. She's an action player and she wants enough action. It's not a question of coming home a winner as of coming home...

B-O-B: Satisfied. Satiated. Fulfilled.

Frank: Yet, you have had incredible success.

Bulletman: The ultimate rush is to go to a casino with plenty of money, knowing that you can really make a killing. Before there were casinos, my thing was to go to a racetrack. Now, I would first go with one-hundred dollars and that was okay. I played cautiously. But the best was when I started going with five-hundred dollars or a thousand dollars. Then I knew I had a chance to really lay it in. I was a threat. That's the ultimate rush. Now, I don't think you've ever experienced that.

Frank: No.

Bulletman: You're much more business-like when you gamble.

B-O-B: I think we're more gamblers than you are. You are serious about it. To us it's a thrill. We get a kick.

Bulletman: We also get a kick about some of the comments you have made in your books that you're happy to leave with a dollar more than when you arrived.

Frank: That's how I feel. A win's a win. I don't really think of myself as a gambler so much as a David going up against a Goliath and, above all, I want to win. The thrill of gambling is secondary to the thrill of winning for me. I don't actually get that much of a thrill from the mere act of gambling.

B-O-B: That's where we are different. Winning is almost irrelevant to us. We do want the action. We're not out of control. We play within our bankroll but we go all out for the big score. That's the difference between you and us.

Frank: Big difference.

B-O-B: To you gambling is a challenge. To us it's a thrill. Your thrill is the challenge, our thrill is …the thrill.

Frank: Makes sense.

B-O-B: To us it's a pleasure. We get tremendous pleasure from gambling.

Bulletman: If we go to Atlantic City for two days and she plays for twelve hours a day, and we go home up or down, it doesn't matter.

B-O-B: I've had the best time. It's not whether I win or lose but the fact that I'm playing the game.

Frank: But you wouldn't think of yourself, yourselves as problem gamblers?

B-O-B: No, I'm actually comfortable going without it for lengths of time because I enjoy the anticipation of a trip too. It's almost as if the anticipation is half the fun. In the winter especially. I have that thing where in the winter you need extra light. Before I discovered gambling, I kid you not, winters were very rough on me. But having a trip to Atlantic City ahead of me, having that to look forward to, helps me tremendously.

Frank: Would you want a casino near you?

B-O-B: I don't think I'd like that. I like the anticipation. If the casino were right here, I don't think I'd like that. I wouldn't want to live in Vegas or Atlantic City because I think it would lose its thrill. I know you can go for two months at a time and play every day but I can't do that.

Frank: Well, I'm very controlled. But the challenge keeps me going. I don't lose that thrill of the challenge no matter how many weeks I've been doing it. And I don't have to win big. Of course, I like winning big but I take it as it comes.

B-O-B: The car ride down to Atlantic City is so much fun. It's who can get up earlier. We giggle, we sing. When we get to New Gretna [an exit that is before Atlantic City on the Garden State Parkway in New Jersey], we'll shout out" "New Grrrreeeetna!"

Bulletman: And then when we get to the Atlantic City Expressway and you see the skyline, you wish you could just tilt the car back, press a button and zing! zoooom! up goes the car into the air and it heads right to the casino!

B-O-B: The ride back is just as much fun. We don't spend all that much time together because he plays craps and I'm glued to the machines. So the ride home we exchange stories. It's all a thrill, really. The socializing, the playing, the dinners, the trips to and from. It's all a part of a thrilling package. We have so much fun.

Frank: Do you ever play anything other than 25 cent joker poker?

B-O-B: I won't play the bigger denominations until I'm ahead a substantial amount. Then I'll move up to dollar machines and sometimes five-dollar machines. But I won't play those machines with what I call "my money." The money I bring with me I consider "my money." The money I win I consider "their money." When I have enough of "their money" I'll take my shot at bigger jackpots on the bigger denomination machines. The few times I've played the five-dollar machines I was too concerned with my bankroll so the game wasn't as enjoyable.

Frank: You weren't in your comfort zone. You get that uneasy feeling when you're playing over your head. Now, let's move on to a topic many players are interested in and that's comps. You and Bulletman are fully comped?

B-O-B: Yes, but it's based on both of our play. Neither one of us alone would merit full RFB [room, food, beverage] but we convinced our host to consider us one person for the purposes of comping. In Atlantic City, you have to bet very large sums to get the full RFB treatment on week-ends but between the two of us we qualify.

Frank: So a husband-wife gambling team should consider talking to a host and gettting themselves considered a single individual?

B-O-B: Definitely. It makes sense from the casino's point of view too. If for example a high roller has a wife who doesn't gamble, he'll still get his comps for two. Two medium rollers will equal the high roller's action so why not get the same treatment? With the competition among casinos, you want your players to stay loyal. This is certainly one way. So we get a nice suite on the weekends with a jacuzzi, nice views, room service, gourmet restaurant and gift shop credits.

Frank: You do have casino loyalty. You tend to go to the same place time and again. Why not try other places?

B-O-B: Well, I have considered at times trying new places but I would have to scout out the machines. It's taken me years to learn which machines are the hitters and which aren't at the casino where I go.

Frank: In Atlantic City, things can be deceptive on video-poker machines. You can't always trust the payout scale to give you a true indication of the percentages because these machines could be programmed with variable programs. So you essentially select machines the way Mr. Handle recommends in *Break the One-Armed Bandits!*

B-O-B: Before I ever knew about Mr. Handle or any of that, I always had a feeling about the machines in Atlantic City. Just from playing as long as I do and as often as I do, I discovered machines that were consistent winners or, if not consistent winners, machines that would hit the progressives. I also know when the progressives have reached their critical mass; when they are about to pop.

Frank: You base this on instinct or analysis?

B-O-B: Partly both. I don't ever play a regular joker-poker machine. I only play the progressives. I've sensed a difference and the progressives in Atlantic City just seem to hit more.

Frank: That's the big scoop of my book. The rules for Atlantic City only stipulate that the sequences must appear in the programming. Let's say that the royal flush comes up once every 40,000 times. In Atlantic City you could have machines that hit this only once every 500,000 times or you could have a machine banging it out once every five or ten thousand times. So what you've sensed on these progressives…these are in-house progressives, yes? Not the ones linked to other casinos?

B-O-B: They are in-house, yes.

Frank: So what you've sensed could very well be true. You have been able through observation and that sixth sense of yours to actually pick the right machines. You could have a whole bank of joker-poker machines, all looking alike, all with the same payout scales, and one or two are programmed to hit like crazy and the others are programmed to be tight as hell. That's because they are actually slot machines and not video poker machines.

B-O-B: I've always felt this. I've always felt that the machines weren't exactly like the video-poker machines in Vegas.

Frank: They're not. Or, at least, they don't have to be.

Bulletman: So strategy decisions would be much more important for Vegas than for Atlantic City?

Frank: Machine selection would be of paramount importance in Atlantic City because you don't know what you're getting. In Vegas, you know what you're getting—unless the casino is cheating. But what would be cheating in Vegas would be abiding by the rules in Atlantic City.

B-O-B: Other players have found this out too. The machines I like to play are heavily played. I have to get to them early and keep them all day because the regulars want them. So I guess without realizing it, people have sensed the same things I have.

Frank: So sum it up for me.

B-O-B: I enjoy going away and when I play my video-poker machines, I go away. It's relaxing and thrilling simultaneously. I also like the solitariness of it. It's just me. I teach sixth graders and I'm on the go all the time in the classroom. I'd say I answer some 400 questions a day. It's a very intense job. I love it but this video-poker gives me a chance to get away and be…

Frank: A hermit?

B-O-B: Something like that. Playing video poker has refreshed me. It makes me ready to deal with the tremendous activity of my regular life.

Frank: Well, I hope you have continued success and I appreciate the fact that you shared with my readers your ideas.

B-O-B: My pleasure.

Three weeks after this chapter was finished and in the hands of my publisher, Angela called me. She had gone on an overnight trip to Atlantic City. In a span of 12 hours she won—hold your breath—three progressive jackpots at three different locations in the same casino. As far as I know, this is an all-time record.

Glossary

Machine Talk

Ace: The highest card in poker, the die with one dot, and another name for a dollar.

Aces and Eights: In poker, this is considered the "dead man's hand" because it was the hand being held by Wild Bill Hickok when he was shot. Also, the name of a version of a video-poker game in honor of Wild Bill.

Ace High: A hand in poker containing odd cards, the highest of which is an ace.

Ace Lock: Brand name for a high security lock found on many slot and video-poker machines that uses a cylindrical key.

Ace Poor: A lower than average number of aces remain in the unplayed cards.

Ace Rich: In blackjack, the composition of the remaining card has more aces proportionally than normal.

Aces Up: A hand in video-poker containing two pair, the higher of which are aces.

Across the Board: A bet on all the numbers (4,5,6,8,9,10) in craps.

Action: The amount of money you wager over a given period of time. Used as a basis of judgment for comps.

Action Player: A player who bets big and for long periods of time. Sometimes used as a euphemism for stupid player.

Ada from Decatur: Archaic craps term for the eight. Sometimes known as Annie from Arkansas.

Adjustable Jackpot: The money compartments of the machine can be adjusted to accommodate a greater or lesser number of coins.

Ante: In poker, chips or cash put up by the players before the dealing of the hands. The ante in video-poker is the money you put in to receive your cards.

Any-craps: A bet at craps that the shooter will roll a two, three, or 12 on the very next roll. A Crazy Crapper bet and not recommended.

Any-Seven: A bet at craps that the next number rolled by the shooter will be a seven. A Crazy Crapper bet and not recommended.

Automatic Payout: Direct payment from the machine to the player without the need of a slot attendant's assistance.

Award Card: Same as *payout card, payment panel, reward card, reward panel, hand payments.* The posted payouts for the various hands of a given video-poker machine.

Back Bonnet: Protective covering in the upper rear portion of a machine.

Backline: A bet on the Don't Pass that the shooter will lose. Any bet that is placed against a shooter.

Back Lip: Protective plate that covers the coin entry area.

Backing the Bet: Placing the odds on the Pass Line and Come bets. One of the better bets in the casino but usually not found in video-poker versions of craps.

Bad Rack: Casinoese for a player who doesn't pay his gambling debts.

Bank: A row of slot or video-poker machines.The person who covers the bet in a game. In most casino gambling, the bank is the casino itself.

Bankroll: The total amount of money a gambler sets aside to gamble with.

Bar: The banning of an individual from playing in a casino—usually at blackjack. Used against cheats and expert players alike. Video-blackjack players don't have to worry about being barred for counting cards as would a table-game player.

Bar the 12 or 2: In craps, the wrong bettor is not allowed to win on these numbers. They are pushes.

Basic Strategy: In blackjack and video blackjack, the best possible play of any given hand based on the dealer's up card and the two cards you possess. In other games, the best play available.

Behind the line: Placing the odds behind your bets on the Pass Line and Come. This is one of the best wagers in the casino. Unfortunately, most versions of video craps do not allow this bet.

Best Buys: Created by the Captain. This radically reduces the house's otherwise stifling edge on these bets. Cannot be employed at video craps however.

Betting against the Dice: In craps, a wager where you are betting against the shooter and for the seven.

Betting with the Dice: At craps, a bet that the shooter will make his point. A bet against the seven showing.

Bias: The tendency of the game to favor either the dealer or the player for prolonged periods.

Big Bertha: Those giant slot machines placed at entrances and exits to lure the unwary gambler. In video poker Big Berthas are usually the Tens-Or-Better variety.

Big Player: At slots or video poker, a player who plays for a sufficient amount of time at a relatively high denomination of machine to receive RFB comps.

Big Six and Big Eight: One of the worst bets at video craps. A wager where you bet that the six or eight will appear before the seven. Pays off at even money. A Crazy Crapper bet.

Blackjack: A natural. A 10-value card and an ace. Pays off at three to two. In video blackjack avoid the machine if blackjack pays even money or three for two.

Board: The tote board that shows the winning keno numbers.

Boxcars: In craps, the number 12.

Box Numbers: The numbers 4, 5, 6, 8, 9, 10.

Break: To go over 21 in blackjack. Sometimes referred to as busting.

Break the Deck: To shuffle the cards before continuing play. Usually in video blackjack, the machine will shuffle before playing out all the cards.

Bug: Sometimes euphemistically called an "odds adjuster." A mechanical contrivance that can be placed on a mechanical slot machine to prevent a given symbol from appearing. The video version of this activity would be called "variable prgramming."

Bull: Another name for the ace in poker.

Bust: To go over 21 in blackjack. Same as breaking.

Bust Out Joint: A casino that cheats the players.

Buy bet: To buy the point numbers four and 10 by paying a five percent commission. Not usually allowed in video craps.

Cage: The cashiers area of a casino where chips and coins are exchanged for cash.

Cancel Button: The button in video poker that allows a player to cancel the previous choice(s) made.

Cancellation Betting System: A betting system using a series of numbers that cancels numbers after a winning bet and adds numbers after a loss. Also known as the *Labouchère system*. Not recommended.

C & E: The abbreviation for craps-eleven. A Crazy Crapper bet that the next roll will be two, three, 11, or 12.

The Captain: The greatest and most innovative craps player in history.

Carousel: The name for an area containing a group of slot machines, usually of the same type, serviced by an individual cashier.

Cash Box: The removable container that accumulates coins.

Cash Out Button: In video poker, the button that allows you to receive the coins that a machine has credited you with.

Casino Advantage: The edge, usually shown as a percentage, that the house has over the player.

Casino Host: The person responsible for seeing that high rollers are treated with the dignity and graciousness their wallets merit.

Casino Manager: The person responsible for seeing that the games of a given casino are handled properly. For machines, this would be a *Slot Manager*.

Centerfield: The name for the nine in craps.

Change Person: Individual who changes currency for coin in the slot areas.

Chasing Losses: Increasing your bets in order to recoup what you've lost. Not a good way to play.

Check: Also known as *token*. The coin that is individually made for each casino that represents the dollar, five-dollar and higher denominations.

Check Rack: The tray that holds the coins for a game.

Choppy Game: A game where neither the house nor the player has been winning consistently. Opposite of a streak.

Clocking: Keeping track of the results of a particular game.

Coin Return: A feature on the slot and video-poker machines that returns either bent coins, tokens from another casino, or slugs to the player.

Cold Dice: Dice that aren't passing or making numbers.

Cold Machine: Any machine where you are losing.

Come Bet: Similar to the Pass Line bet, a wager that the next point number rolled will come up before another seven is thrown.

Come Out Roll: The roll that establishes the shooter's Pass Line point.

Come Point: The come number that must be repeated before a seven is thrown.

Comp: The "freebies" that casinos give out for certain levels of betting.

Cradle: Sometimes referred to as a "sensing cradle." Where newly played coins come to rest for the purposes of "sensing." If the coin is present and acceptable, play will proceed.

Crapless Craps: New game where the two, three, 11, and 12 become point numbers.

Crap Out: To roll a two, three or 12 on the come out roll.

Craps: The numbers two, three, and 12.

Crazy Crapper bets: The Captain's term for all the bad bets in craps.

Credit Button: On slot and video-poker machines, the button that allows the player to play winning credits and not coin. You can play one credit or any number of credits up to the maximum.

Credit Line: The amount of credit a player is allowed by a given casino.

Credit Manager: The person in charge of determining casino credit for a player.

Crossroader: A casino cheat.

Day shift: The casino work shift that usually runs from 10 am to 6 pm.

Dead Hand: In video poker, a hand that has been discarded or can no longer be made.

Deal Button: In video poker, the button that is pushed to get the machine to "deal" the cards.

Dealer-in-the-machine: The random-number generator that selects "at random" the next cards to be dealt.

Denomination: A machine's classification based upon what type of coin is required to play it. Denominations can range from five cents to five-hundred dollars.

Deuces: The two in cards and the two on the dice.

Devil: A term for the seven in craps. "The devil jumped up!"

Dice: Cubes with six sides, numbered respectively one through six.

Die: One cube, the singular form of dice.

Discretionary Removal: The ability in place betting to call off or remove your bets. Odds bets are also discretionary. So are Don't Come, Don't Pass bets.

Do Bet: To bet with the dice and against the seven.

Doey-Don't: An element of the Captain's *Supersystem.* Cannot be played on video-craps games.

Don't Bet: To bet against the dice and for the seven.

Don't Come: A bet at craps that the next point number rolled will not be repeated before a seven is thrown. One of the better bets in the casino.

Don't Pass: A bet at craps that the shooter will not make his point before the seven is thrown.

Double Down: In blackjack, to double the size of your bet and receive only one card. You can also double for less than the initial wager.

Double Exposure: Blackjack game where both of the dealer's cards are dealt face up.

Double Odds: The right to place a free odds bet up to double the original Pass Line or Come bet. One of the best bets in the casino. Rarely found in video craps.

Double Progressive Video Poker: Two different progressive video-poker jackpots on the same machines, each growing independently. Jackpots alternate based on pull of the handle or press of the button.

Double Up System: This is also known as the Martingale family of wagers. Player attempts to get all his previous losses back by increasing (doubling) his previous bet.

Draw: In video poker, to receive new cards.

Draw Button: The button on a video-poker machine that allows a player to receive another card.

Drilling: A cheating method whereby the cheat drills a hole in themachine in order to manipulate or freeze the reels in a jackpot position.

Dumping: A machine that is losing money to the players.

Duplicate ticket: The receipt for a regular keno ticket given to a player after he places his bet. Also known as an *outside ticket.*

Early surrender: Rarely found rule in blackjack that allowed players to forfeit half their bet, even if the dealer had a blackjack.

Easy way: In craps, the numbers four, six, eight, and 10 made without doubles.

Edge: Having the advantage in a game.

Eighty-six: The same as barring someone from playing in the casino.

Escalator: A device that displays, usually for identification of slugs, the coins most recently put into the machine.

Even Up: A bet that has no mathematical edge for either side.

Even Money: A bet that pays off at one to one.

Eye in the Sky: The cameras, usually in bubbles, located throughout the casino that videotape the action.

Face Cards: The king, queen and jack. Also known as *picture cards* or *paint*.

Fair Game: A game where neither the house nor the player has an edge.

Favorable Deck: A deck whose remaining cards favors the player.

Field Bet: A wager at craps that wins if the number two, three, four, nine, 10, 11, or 12 is rolled. Shooter loses on a five, six, seven, and eight.

5-Count: The revolutionary system developed by the Captain to avoid horrendous rolls of the dice, stretch the amount of time your money gives you at the table, and position you to take advantage of hot rolls. A modified version of this might be possible at video-craps.

Flat Bet: Bet that is paid off at even money in craps. Also, any player who bets the same amount hand after hand.

Flattop Machines: Fixed, maximum payout machines.

Fluctuation in Probability: Numbers or cards appearing out of all proportion to their probability. A short sequence of repeating numbers. A mathematical term that means good or bad luck depending on whether the fluctuation is in your favor or not.

Flush: In poker, five cards of the same suit.

Fold: In poker, to drop out of play.

Four Flush: Four of the same suit. A four-flusher was someone who attempted to win a pot by declaring a flush when he only had four of the same suit.

Four of a Kind: Four cards of the same rank.

Four Straight: Four cards in sequence.

Free Play: To be able to play a slot machine or video-poker machine without having to put in coins.

Free Odds: Wager placed behind the Pass Line bet or the Come bet that is paid off at the true odds. Usually not avilable in video craps.

Front Line: Another name for the Pass Line in craps.

Front Money: Money previously deposited with the cage and used by the player to draw markers against.

Full House: A poker hand consisting of three of a kind and two of a kind.

Full Odds: Whatever the maximum odds allowed on a given craps table. Option not usually available in video craps.

Fun Book: Coupon book used by casinos to encourage play. Can be used to get an advantage at certain games if two players pool money and bet opposite sides. Also, contains discounts for drinks, food, etc.

Future Pay Machines: A type of machine that holds back the payout until the next play.

Gaffed: Any gaming device that has been rigged.

Gambling Stake: Amount of money reserved for gambling. Same as bankroll.

George: A good tipper.

Grand Martingale: A wagering system where you double your bets and add one extra unit after a loss.

Graveyard Shift: The 2 AM to 10 AM working shift in a casino.

Grifter: A scam artist.

Grind: Derogatory term for low roller. A small-money player. Term for long-term effects of the slight casino edge on a player's bankroll.

Grind Down: The casino winning all of a player's money due to the advantage it has on bets.

Grind Joint: A casino that caters to low rollers.

Grind System: Increasing one's bet by a unit after each win. Also, any system that attempts to win small amounts frequently against the casinos.

Guerrilla Gambling: The combination of smart play and hit-and-run tactics to beat the casinos at their own games. See my book, *Guerrilla Gambling: How to Beat the Casinos at Their own Games!*

Gutshot Straight: In Video Poker, a straight that can only be made by drawing a single card. Same as an *inside straight*.

Hand: A player's cards in a card game. Also, the entire series of rolls in a craps game by one shooter.

Hard Hand: Any blackjack hand without an ace or a blackjack hand that cannot use the ace as an 11.

Hardway Bets: A bet in craps that the shooter will roll the four, six, eight, or 10 as doubles before a seven shows. A Crazy Crapper bet.

Hardway Hop: A bet that the shooter will roll a particular total as doubles on the very next roll. A Crazy Crapper bet. Not usually found on video craps.

Head to Head: To play against the dealer with no other player in the game. Sometimes referred to as *face to face*, or *heads up*. Many video blackjack games are "head-to-head" contests vs. the dealer-in-the-machine.

Heat: Surveillance by the casino of a suspected card counter. Or pressure put on a card counter to leave before being banned. Also, known as *steam*. Not a problem for video-blackjack players.

High Card: A jack, queen, king or ace.

High-Low: A bet at craps that the next roll will be a two or a 12. Also, different spelling for the counting system Hi-Lo in blackjack.

High Roller: A player who plays for large stakes.

High Roller System: A method of betting for large stakes developed by the Captain that reduces the house edge and allows excellent comps without the normal risk. Would include the *best buys*. Cannot be done at video craps.

High Pair: A pair of jacks, queens, kings or aces.

Hit: To receive another card on your hand in blackjack.

Hold: The actual amount that the casinos take from their games. To save certain cards.

Hold Button: In video poker, the button that allows you to keep certain cards.

Hole Card: The second card dealt to the dealer in blackjack, that is face down. Any face down card.

Hop: A bet in craps that the next roll of the dice will be a certain combination. A Crazy Crapper bet. Usually not available at video craps.

Hopper: Electronically powered payout system that counts out the coins to be paid accurately and fast. Some people also use the term hopper to refer to the tray that catches the coins.

Horn Bet: A one roll bet in craps that combines the two, three, 11 and 12.

Horn High: A horn bet at craps where one of the totals has one more unit riding on it than all the others.

Horrendous Rolls: Rolls where the shooter sevens out within a few rolls after establishing his point number.

Hot: A player who has been winning.

Hot and Cold System: A wager on the side that won previously. Another name for the streak method of betting.

Hot Dice: Dice that have been passing and making numbers.

Hot Machine: A machine where the players have been winning.

Hot Shooter: A shooter having a good roll at the craps table.

House Edge: The mathematical edge that the casino has on a given bet or machine.

House Odds: The payoff that reflects the casino's tax on your winning bet.

Hustler: A gambling cheat.

Inside Numbers: In craps, the numbers five, six, eight, nine.

Inside straight: A straight that can only be completed by one card on the inside. Example: 4-5- * -7-8.

Insurance: A side wager at blackjack for up to half the original wager that the dealer has a blackjack when he has an ace showing.

Irregularity: A departure from the standard procedures at a given game.

Jackpot: A grand payout, either on a machine or at a table game.

Jackpot Jumpers: Name for the thieves who attempt to steal your jackpot either by claiming it was theirs or by befriending you and making off with your money when you least suspect it.

Johnson Act: A federal law that forbids the shipment of gambling devices except to states that can operate them legally. Act took effect on January 3, 1951.

Joker: A wild card that can usually be used as a substitute for any card in the deck. Usually resembles a court jester.

Juice: The five percent commission that the house charges on buy bets in craps. Not available on video craps. Also known as *vig* or *vigorish.*

Junket: A trip arranged, organized and subsidized by a casino to bring gamblers to play at the games.

Junket master: The person in charge of a junket.

Kelly Criterion: A betting system utilizing the knowledge of a player's advantage at any given point in the game. The player bets the proportion of his bankroll that represents his advantage.

Kibitzer: An individual who is not playing at a given game but is giving unwanted advice.

Kicker: In poker, an extra card, usually a high card, that is kept with a pair. Not a good strategy in video poker.

Law of Repeating Numbers: The Captain's tongue-in-cheek term for his observation that numbers tend to repeat during short-term fluctuations.

Lay Bet: A wrong bet on a number at craps that is paid off at true odds after the casino extracts a five percent commission.

Laying Odds: For the wrong bettor to make an odds bet on the Don't Pass or the Don't Come. Not available in video craps.

Layout: The design imprinted with the various bets at a given game.

Level One System: Any card counting system that uses +1 or -1 as the value of the cards that are counted.

Levels: Honest gaming equipment and personnel. As in: "This game is on the level."

Liberty Bell: The original slot machine created by Charles Fey.

Light-Up Slot Machines: First created by the Jennings Company. Machines that have electronically lit panels.

Limited Bankroll System: The name of the craps system for individuals who can't afford the Captain's best buys, or who do not wish to play the *Supersystem* or *5-Count* Pass and Come. Also known as the *Low Roller System.* A version of this system can be played at video craps.

Line Bet: A bet in craps on the pass line.

Little Joe: In craps, a roll of four. Also called *Little Joe from Kokomo.*

Long end of a bet: The side of a bet that must pay off more than it collects.

Long Run: The concept that a player could play so often that probability would tend to even out. That is, you would start to see the total appearance of numbers approximating what probability theory predicts. A long run player is one who plays a lot!

Loose Machine: A slot machine or video-poker machine that is paying off more than other machines of its type. A machine that is winning for a player.

Low Hand: In video poker, any non-paying hand.

Low Pair: In video poker, any pair that doesn't win money on the payout schedule.

Making a point: Having your Pass Line number repeat before the appearance of a seven.

Mark: An individual who has been or is going to be cheated. A sucker.

Marker: The check a player fills out before receiving casino credit at a table. A promissory note or I.O.U.

Martingale system of wagering: Doubling one's bet after a loss in an attempt to make back all your losses and a small win.

Mechanical Machine: The oldest form of gaming device. Ran by gears, pulleys, an levers. The handle was the direct cause of all that happened inside the machine.

Megapoker: Giant inter-casino linked-progressive video-poker machines that pay out huge jackpots for specific hands.

Microprocessor Machines: The modern, computerized "smart" machines, where a microprocessor computer chip controls and simulates play action.

Money at Risk: Money that has been wagered and can be lost.

Money Management: The methods a player uses to conserve his bankroll from ruin.

Monster roll: A craps roll that is long and where many numbers and points are rolled. The dream of every craps player. The "Arm" from *Beat the Craps Out of the Casinos* is known as the Queen of the Monsters for the epic rolls she regularly produces.

Multiple-Coin Machine (Multipliers): Slot and video poker machines that require more than one coin for maximum payouts.

Multiple-Deck game: Blackjack played with more than one deck which gives the house more of an advantage over the player.

Multiple Hands: To play more than one hand at blackjack. Some video-blackjack machines allow this.

Multiple-Pay Machines: Machines that pay out on more than one line depending on how many coins you put in.

Nail: To catch someone cheating. "We nailed him."

Natural: A perfect hand. In blackjack, an ace and a 10 card. In craps, a seven or 11 on the come-out roll.

Negative Count: A count at blackjack that favors the casino.

Negative Progression: Any system of wagering where you increase bets after a loss.

Nickel: A five dollar chip or coin.

Non-Seven Mode: A roll in which a rhythmic roller is positioning and rolling the dice in such a way that the seven doesn't appear. Unfortunately, unless a machine is faulty, tis is not a considereation in video craps.

N.S.G.N.G.R: The Captain's tongue-in-cheek rule that you should never get upset ifyou can't guess correctly for example, at video keno. Stands for *No Second Guess No Guess Rule.*

Nut: The total amount of money needed to run a casino or the total amount of money an individual needs to succeed at what he is doing.

Odds: The bet that pays off at true odds in craps. Not availble in video poker. Also, the likelihood of a given event happening.

Off: To remove a bet from play at craps for one or more rolls. Means no decision will affect that bet.

On: All your bets are working or at risk on the next roll.

One-Armed Bandits: The term given to slot machines at a time when they were sold and distributed by less-than-reputable individuals.

One Roll Bet: A bet that will be decided on the very next roll of the dice. All one roll bets are Crazy Crapper bets and should be avoided.

One Roll Hardway: The next roll will be a four, six, eight or 10 made with doubles. Usually not available at video craps.

On the Square: A game that is honest.

Outside numbers: The box numbers four, five, nine and 10 on the craps layout.

Paint: A picture card. When a player says, "Paint me," he wants a picture card.

Pair: In poker, two cards of the same denomination.

Parallel Dealing: In video poker, cards are dealt with their replacement cards already behind them. When you discard initial card, the replacement card is revealed.

Parlay: To double one's bet after a win.

Pass: A win by a shooter at craps, either on the come out roll or by making his point.

Pass Line: A wager with the shooter that he will make his point.

Pat Hand: Any hand in a card game that does not require getting additional cards.

Patience System: A grind method of playing whereby the player waits for a certain number of decisions before placing a bet. The Captain's methods of play all require a certain amount of patience.

Payline: The line upon which a player is paid at slots. Generally corresponds to the number of coins played.

Payout Meter: A numerical counter with a visible display that keeps a running count of the coins played and paid out after each win.

Payout Percentage: The percentage of the money played that is returned to the player.

P.C.: The house edge expressed as a percentage.

Penetration: How deeply a dealer deals into a deck or a shoe at blackjack.

Penny Ante: A game played for small stakes.

Pilgrim's Progression: The Captain's method for getting more money on the table during a hot roll. To be used in the High Roller System. A limited version of this could be used in video craps. See my book, *Beat the Craps Out of the Casinos: How to Play Craps and Win!*

Place Bet: In craps, going directly up on a number. The house pays the bet at house odds and not true odds. Usually not available at video craps.

Plus-Minus System: Another name for the Hi-Lo system or High-Low system of card counting. Cards are given a +1 or a-1 value.

Playing Cycle: The sequence of events that occurs from the moment a player puts in the coins to the moment a decision is rendered.

Point: The number (four, five, six, eight, nine or 10) which the shooter must repeat before a seven is rolled in order to win on the Pass Line at craps.

Pokermania: Vide-poker version of Quartermania. An inter-casino, progressive-linked jackpot that ontinues to grow until a player hits it.

Positive Count: A count at blackjack that favors the player.

Power of the Pen (or Pencil): The ability to issue hotel comps to players on the part of some casino executives.

Premium players: A casino term meaning big bettors or players with big credit lines.

Press: To increase the amount wagered, usually by doubling it, after a win.

Price: The total sum wagered on a keno ticket. Also, the house percentage on a given bet.

Producer: Casino term for a player who losses often and for large sums. This individual is a producer of profits for the casino.

Progressive Jackpots: The grand prize offered on certain kinds of slot and video poker machines that keeps growing as more and more money is played. Grows until it is hit by a player.

Proposition Bet: Bets in the center of the craps layout. These are all Crazy Crapper bets and should be avoided. Also, any bet that is a longshot and carries a heavy house edge.

Push: Casinoese for tie.

Pushing the House or Pushing the Casino: The term coined by the Captain to describe a player in the act of getting a better game from a casino than advertised. For example, the *best buy* bets have radically pushed the casinos. Not possible at most video games.

Quarter Player: A player who plays exclusively on quarter machines.

Random Number Generator: Sometimes referred to by its initials, RNG. The computer program hat generates a series of random numbers. In microprocessor machines, each sequence of random numbers will correspond to a specific card in video poker.

Rating: Evaluating a player's play for the purpose of comps.

RFB: Complimentary room, food and beverage.

Rhythmic Roller: A shooter who by chance or design gets into a non-seven mode. Usually a shooter who rolls the dice the same way time after time. This won't be encountered in video craps since the shooter-in-the-machine is a program and not a person.

Rich Deck: In blackjack, a deck that has many 10 value cards remaining to be played.

Right Bettor: A player who bets with the dice and against the seven.

Royal Flush: An ace, king, queen, jack and 10 of the same suit.

Ruin or Element of Ruin: Losing your bankroll. The probability of losing every penny of your bankroll.

Rule Card: The card that shows the rules for a given game.

Running Count: In blackjack, the raw count that has not been divided (or multipled) by the number of decks remaining.

Rush: A quick winning streak.

Scam: Any scheme to defraud a casino or player.

Scared Money: Money a player can't afford to lose. Also known as perspiration pennies.

Secondary Decision Programming: A type of programming that allows the computer to stop a hand that is about to be dealt in favor of a different hand. This is done to prevent big winning hands from appearing their theoretical number of times. One of the methods used for cheating or "fixing" a video-poker machine to have it perform as a slot machine. Also called variable programming.

Serial Dealing: In video poker the cards will be dealt as they come off the top of the deck. When you discard a card, the replacement card has not already been selected but will be the next card off the top of the deck. This is the opposite of parallel dealing.

Session: A given period of play at a casino. Usually terminated at a predetermined time, or at a certain level of wins or losses.

Seven Out: For a shooter at craps to roll a seven before repeating his point number.

Shift Boss: The individual in charge of the casino during a given work shift.

Shoot: To roll the dice.

Shooter: The person who rolls the dice. In video craps, it's the machine's programing that rolls the "dice."

The Short End: The side of a bet that has to pay off less than it will win.

Short Odds: Less than the true odds payoff of a bet.

Short Run: The limited amount of time during any given session when probability theory will seemingly be skewed by streaks or fluctuations.

Shuffle up: Technique used to thwart card counters. Dealer will shuffle after every deal or when a player enters a game and bets big money. Can't be employed at video blackjack.

Single-Deck Blackjack: The best game in the casino if the rules are standard. Most video-blackjack games are single-deck games.

Single Odds: The ability of a player to place an amount equal to his Pass Line or Come bet in odds that will be paid off at the true odds for the number. Usually not avilable at video craps.

Sleeper: A winning bet at craps that the player has forgotten about. Quite often the player will leave a table and the bet will remain until it is lost or some player or dealer takes it. Sleeper bets can be found on machines when players fail to cash out their credits at the end of play

Slot Arcade: A casino devoted exclusively to slot machines and video-poker machines.

Slot Floor: Areas devoted to slot machines in a casino.

Slot Mix: Slot machines and video-poker machines of different denominations and of different percentages in the slot area.

Slug: A group of cards that have been prearranged in a given order. Also, a piece of rounded metal inserted into a slot machine that mimics a coin.

Snake Eyes: The two at craps.

Snapper: An archaic term for a blackjack. A red snapper is a blackjack composed of two red cards.

Soft hand: A hand at blackjack where the ace can be used as 11.

Split: To make two hands from a pair at blackjack.

Spooning: Sticking a spoon into a slot machine to get it to pay off. Doesn't work on new machines.

Spot: The number on a keno ticket that has been "X"-ed out for betting purposes.

Spread: The difference between the minimum and maximum bets a player makes.

Squares: A game or player that is honest. "This game is on the square."

Stand: To keep the cards you have. Not to draw any more cards.

Steaming: A player who is visibly upset and is playing recklessly.

Stiff: In blackjack, a total of 12 through 16. Also, not to tip a cocktail server.

Straight: Five cards in sequence.

Straight Flush: Five cards of the same suit in sequence.

Straight Ticket: A keno ticket that has only one wager and that involves the selection of from one to 15 different numbers.

Stringing: A method of cheating whereby a coin or slug suspended on a string is introduced time and again ino a machine in order to get free play.

Surrender: A blackjack option where the player may give up half his bet. Player loses full bet if the dealer has a blackjack, however. Sometimes known as late surrender.

Supersystem: The method of play developed by the Captain for long-term play at craps. Divided into the classical and radical supersystems. Can't be used in video craps.

Sweat: Casinos who are upset by players winning are said to "sweat" out their games. Also, a player who is losing and is worried.

Swing Shift: The shift that runs from 6 PM to 2 AM.

Take the Edge: Giving yourself an edge at a game—usually by cheating. A player can take the edge at certain video-poker games and video-blackjack games.

Taking the odds: To put the odds behind a Pass Line or a Come bet. Usually canot be made at video craps.

Tapped Out: To lose one's entire bankroll.

Three Flush: Three cards to a flush.

Three of a Kind: Having three cards of the same denomination.

Three Straight: Three cards to a straight.

Tight machine: A slot machine that is not paying back a good percentage. A machine that a player is losing at.

Tilting: Any physical manipulation of machine during play in order to influence the outcome.

Toke: A tip to a casino employee.

Tom: Casinoese for a poor tipper.

Tough Out: The Captain's term for a skilled player who doesn't beat himself.

Triple Odds: The placing of three times one's original bet in odds behind the Pass Line or Come bets. Usually not available at video craps.

True Count: The adjusted count at blackjack that reflects the count per remaining decks.

True Odds: The actual probability of an event happening.

Twenty-One: Another name for blackjack.

Two Pair: A hand at poker consisting of two separate pairs.

Underground Joint: An illegal casino.

Unfavorable Deck: A deck in blackjack that favors the casino.

Up Card: Any card that is dealt face up.

Variable Programming: A type of programming that allows the computer to stop a hand that is about to be dealt in favor of a different hand. This is done to prevent big winning hands from appearing their theoretical number of times. One of the methods used for cheatingor "fixing" a video-poker machine to have it perform as a slot machine.

Vic: A sucker. Short for victim.

Vig or Vigorish: The casino tax on a bet. Also known as juice.

Virgin Principle: The superstition that a beginner will have luck. Also known as beginner's luck.

Volatility: The tendency of a video-poker game to have many losing sessions punctuated by explosive winning sessions.

Wager: Another term for a bet.

Wash: One bet cancels out another bet.

Wild Card: A card that can be used for any other card in a game.

Working Bet: A bet at craps that is at risk.

Wrong Bettor: A player who bets against the shooter and with the seven.

Appendix

Recommended Reading

Video poker has come a long way since it was lumped with slots as a mindless diversion for the wives, companions, trophy-dates of serious gamblers. Of course, the definition of a serious gambler was a person who played table games, preferably for large stakes. But all that has changed thanks largely to a small coterie of gaming authors who first brought to the public's attention the fact that certain varieties of video poker could be beaten. If you are serious about becoming a great video-poker player, you owe it to yourself to make the acquaintence of the following authors. Each has his own style of writing, approach to the game, and philosophy of gaming. What they have in common is a serious approach to the subject of video poker. The strategies of these authors for like machines will vary little if at all. That is as it should be. A computer generates the results after all and there aren't many diverse ways of interpreting these results. Essentially and strategically, you will not learn anything "new" from reading the works of the writers listed here but don't let that stop you. There is such a thing as wisdom in gambling and the accumulated knowledge of the following gaming authors will put you on the path to video-poker wisdom.

Lenny Frome: The dean of American video-poker writers and a cottage industry, Lenny Frome was the first author to recognize that video poker could be beaten. I highly recommend his *Video Poker: America's National Game of Chance and his Winning Strategies for Video Poker*. But all his stuff is excellent. When new machines come on the scene Mr. Frome is usually the first to do a detailed analysis and narrative of them - much to the casinos' collective chagrin. Mr. Frome writes for many gambling publications and he'll be happy to send you information on his offerings. Write him C/O Compu-Flyers (425); 5025 S. Eastern Ave. (16) Las Vegas, NV 89119

Bradley Davis: Davis is an interesting and compelling author because he is a Joker Poker fanatic. This he couples with a religious sensibility that makes for a good read. His *Mastering Joker Wild Video Poker* is an exhausting and fascinating study of all aspects of this one particular variation of video poker. If your game is Joker Poker, you should definitely read Mr. Davis. Write him C/O Applied Technology Press, PO Box 460565, Aurora, CO 80046-0565.

Dan Paymar: Another ground-breaking video-poker author whose newsletter *The Video Poker Times* is a must read for the serious player. A good writer with an encompassing and pleasing style, Paymar does detailed analyses of every type of game. His booklet, *Video Poker: Precision Play*, is another must read. Make sure when you order it you ask for the latest updated issue since Mr. Paymar constantly adds and subtracts from the booklet as events warrant. Write him C/O Enhanceware, 2413 S. Eastern Avenue, Suite 121, Las Vegas, NV 89104

Recommended Newsletters

Blackjack Forum, published by Arnold Snyder, contains useful articles on video poker contributed by Dan Paymar plus occasional but extremely detailed examinations of video blackjack. Although this is primarily a newsletter for serious card counters in blackjack, there is enough information here to make it a good purchase for the video-poker and video-blackjack player. It was this publication's articles on video blackjack that put me on to the scent for my expose of Atlantic City machines. The writing in this publication is uniformly excellent. For subscription information write to: RGE, 414, Santa Clara Ave., Oakland, CA 94610

Chance and Circumstance, published by Paone Press, contains my ruminations on this gambling life. I first broke my findings on video-poker machines in this quarterly newsletter. It was here I delineated my theory of beating the casinos' slot machines by using the casinos' own computers to discover the exact locations of "loose" and "tight" slots. The thrust of this publication is gaming in general and my observations in particular. Occasionally, I'll have guest writers and the Captain is a regular contributor. Subscription is $50 for one year. Write Paone Press, Box 610, Lynbrook, NY 11563.

Index

Best Bets from Bonus Books

Break the One-Armed Bandits
How to come out ahead when you play the slots
Frank Scoblete
ISBN 1-56625-001-3
178 pages—paper—$9.95

Beat the Craps out of the Casinos
How to play craps and win
Frank Scoblete
ISBN 0-929387-34-1
152 pages—paper—$9.95

Guerrilla Gambling
How to beat the casinos at their own games
Frank Scoblete
ISBN 1-56625-027-7
339 pages—paper—$12.95

Workouts and Maidens
Inside betting info for those who want to win at the track
Vincent Reo
ISBN 1-56625-000-5
180 pages—paper—$11.95

Finding HOT Horses
Picking horses that can win for you
Vincent Reo
ISBN 0-929387-96-1
135 pages—paper—$12.00

Overlay, Overlay: How to Bet Horses Like a Pro
Leading trainers and jockeys share their handicapping secrets
Bill Heller
ISBN 0-933893-86-8
228 pages—paper—$9.95

Harness Overlays: Beat the Favorite
We'll show you how
Bill Heller
ISBN 0-929387-97-X
139 pages—paper—$12.00

Woulda, Coulda, Shoulda
"Best introduction to horse racing ever written"—*Thoroughbred Times*
Dave Feldman with Frank Sugano
ISBN 0-933893-02-3
281 pages—paper—$9.95

Bonus Books, Inc., 160 East Illinois Street, Chicago, Illinois 60611

TOLL-FREE: 800 • 225 • 3775   **FAX: 312 • 467 • 9271**